Praise for *How We Grow Through What We Go Through*

"Chris Willard's latest book offers a straightforward yet science-based guide to recovery and healing, from the individual to the collective."

—EMMA SEPPÄLÄ, Yale psychologist and author of *The Happiness Track*

"Dr. Willard has written an accessible book that gives beautiful context to the complexities of what happens inside of our bodies and in our relationships with one another when we undergo the experience of rupture and trauma, both individually and collectively. He lays out a compassionate road map for how we might find growth and the reemergence of possibility through it all. During a time when people are desperately looking for a way to understand their own relationship to mental, emotional, and physical pain and how it is impacted by our intersectional identities so as to be empowered to heal themselves and the planet, this book will prove to be a very helpful guide and resource to help us restore our capacity to treat ourselves and one another with loving-awareness."

—DR. SARÁ KING, neuroscientist, medical anthropologist, education philosopher, and founder of MindHeart Consulting

"A beacon in this era of our collective trauma that lights a way back into our bodies to reclaim our growth."

—PATRICK TEAHAN, LICS

"Dr. Willard's Attend and Befriend approach to recovering from stress and trauma unfailingly normalizes the reader's distress and skillfully encourages the recovery of innate capacities to experience enough safety inside one's self to feel safe again in the world. What sets this book apart is the unpretentious way Dr. Willard walks with the reader step-by-step through the science and a workable sequence of practices that empower the reader to both heal through post-traumatic stress and heal into post-traumatic growth.

"I especially appreciate the author's sensitivity to the realities of marginalized groups and the empathic sharing of so many stories of real people who show us that we, too, can learn to act our way into new feelings, new thoughts, new possibilities for our lives."

—LINDA GRAHAM, MFT, author of *Resilience: Powerful Practices for Bouncing Back from Disappointment, Difficulty, and Even Disaster*

"With love and rigor, Chris Willard has offered us an invaluable road map to working skillfully with trauma. The writing is thoughtful, the practices are accessible, and the message is exactly what we need: that we can survive (and even thrive) when faced with traumatic stress. Highly recommended!"

—DAVID TRELEAVEN, PHD, author of *Trauma-Sensitive Mindfulness: Practices for Safe and Transformative Healing*

"As we emerge from this global pandemic — into still more instability and trauma, we are beginning to understand the impact it has had on all of our bodies, hearts and minds. Collective healing is possible when we remember how deeply our lives are intertwined and that we belong to each other."

—LESLIE BOOKER, co-author of *Best Practices for Yoga in a Criminal Justice Setting*

"Dr. Chris Willard provides a profound and restorative guide to the nonlinear journey that is healing from trauma. He offers nuanced language for understanding the impact of trauma on the nervous system and what it means to befriend, reset, and reregulate while honoring the many intersections and layers of our lived experience. Dr. Willard wrote this book in a way that is accessible, affirming, academic, and empowering while also making you feel like you are sitting with a friend over coffee and reflecting on your resilience. A one-of-a-kind resource that honors and centers the humanity of all those who have experienced trauma. A must-read for mental health and healing professionals inspired to integrate an understanding of neuroscience, mindfulness, self-compassion, and embodiment into their work with clients."

—ZAHABIYAH YAMASAKI, MED, RYT, author of *Trauma-Informed Yoga for Survivors of Sexual Assault* and forthcoming children's book *Your Joy is Beautiful*

HOW
WE GROW
THROUGH
WHAT
WE GO
THROUGH

CHRISTOPHER WILLARD, PsyD

HOW WE GROW THROUGH WHAT WE GO THROUGH

Self-Compassion Practices
for Post-Traumatic Growth

sounds true
BOULDER, COLORADO

Sounds True
Boulder, CO 80306

Published 2022

Cover design by Mia Cupidro
Book design by Meredith Jarrett
Illustrations on pages 12–13 by Juliet Percival

Printed in Canada

BK006364

Names: Willard, Christopher (Psychologist), author.
Title: How we grow through what we go through : self-compassion
    practices for post-traumatic growth / by Christopher Willard, PsyD.
Description: Boulder, CO : Sounds True, 2022. | Includes
    bibliographical references.
Identifiers: LCCN 2022013159 (print) | LCCN 2022013160 (ebook)
    | ISBN 9781683648901 (trade paperback) | ISBN 9781683648918
    (ebook)
Subjects: LCSH: Self-actualization (Psychology) | Mindfulness
    (Psychology) | Resilience (Personality trait) | Mind and body.
Classification: LCC BF637.S4 W4944 2022
    (print) | LCC BF637.S4 (ebook) | DDC
    158.1--dc23/eng/20220715
LC record available at https://lccn.loc.
    gov/2022013159
LC ebook record available at https://lccn.loc.
    gov/2022013160

10 9 8 7 6 5 4 3 2 1

Contents

Preface

This book emerged in the midst of the first year of the COVID-19 pandemic, while forests and cities burned, as climate change accelerated, and as a critical and historic presidential election loomed on the horizon. Such times of personal and global upheaval unsettle and even rewire our individual and collective nervous systems, often in ways that are deeply traumatic. And yet, it's not like the rest of life stopped happening in 2020. Close friends lost jobs. My son's best friend moved across the country. My mom got diagnosed with a rare, degenerative dementia called Lewy body dementia, a heartbreaking spiral into physical paralysis and memory loss. She died weeks after vaccines became available. Life and death and their ten thousand joys and sorrows continued apace, only there was a pandemic to contend with, too.

Friday the thirteenth of March, 2020, was the day that everything shut down where my family lives. Passengers on my flight home from Chicago had been wearing masks and gloves, and suddenly our kids' school was canceled for the next two weeks. (Remember when

pandemic closures were going to be for only two weeks?)
The entire globe seemed to skid into a sudden stop.

My wife and I sat on the back porch, looking into our postage stamp–sized yard as the kids trampled through the lingering snow. We actually had a moment to chat as we sipped our coffee and the kids entertained themselves for once.

"The kids are never going to forget this time," I uttered, trying to sound profound. My wife—a medical historian whose job is literally to study the ways that plagues and pandemics alter the course of history—glanced over at me, one eye still on the kids. "No one is going to forget this time," she said. "Historians will talk about the coronavirus pandemic of 2020 [and then the delta variant of 2021 and the omicron variant of 2022] in a thousand years."

I sat and pondered this as the kids began creating an imaginary ice cream shop with the muddy snow. *How do I want them to remember this time?* I wondered. *How do I want them to remember me in this time? How do I want to feel when I remember this time?* The questions nagged at me for the rest of the afternoon.

Later, when I found myself panic-buying eight pounds of dried garbanzo beans, I reflected, *Do I want to be the guy who bought the last roll of toilet paper, or the guy who dropped off a few extra rolls at our elderly neighbor's house? And I guess I can be the guy who drops off hummus*

for the neighbors, too, since I bought way too many beans.
Then, as my own mother went in and out of the hospital at the height of the first COVID-19 surge, I asked myself *What kind of son do I want to be when my mother is sick?* Although friends on social media were running marathons on their home treadmills or learning five new languages during lockdown, the conversations *I* had with friends and clients became less about what we were going to *do* in this time and more about who we wanted to *be* throughout the pandemic and after.

Who do I want to be? nagged me throughout that time when billions of people around the world stopped what they were doing to "shelter in place" and recognized for the first time that "essential workers" toiled on in fear of infection. Some people's lives changed little; most changed a lot. Some experienced the trauma of death and dying up close with family and friends. Others said goodbye to loved ones over iPads. Millions lost jobs, homes, careers, and educations. Domestic violence surged as people abused substances and each other. In the midst of all of it, new waves of civil rights protests broke out, first in Minneapolis and then around the nation and the world as attention turned to another pandemic—one of racism, injustice, and violence against African Americans that has persisted for generations. I kept reflecting, *What kind of ally have I been? What kind of ally do I want to be going forward?* My choices followed and flowed from these questions, and they led me here.

This book is my answer to those questions—or maybe it's more accurate to say my "response" to these questions. As individuals, as communities, as humans, we can allow traumas to push us toward more sickness, sadness, fear, and division—or we can use them to water the seeds of our growth and development. Post-traumatic stress disorder (PTSD) gets a lot of press, but the reality is that PTG, or post-traumatic growth, is the far more likely outcome of life's challenges.

In my research I've discovered the foundations of PTG not just in neuroscience and psychology, but in anthropology and in human history. We can change and grow. We can access the tools built into our bodies to become more resilient and empowered. We can train our minds and hearts, growing new connections in our brains through the wonder of neuroplasticity.

Neuroplasticity describes the way the brain physically "rewires" and changes in response to how we use it and to the experiences we have. To paraphrase Canadian neuropsychologist Donald Hebb, "Neurons that fire together, wire together." Study after study shows that we can change our brains through meditation and other practices, much the way we build muscle through regular exercise.

We can change our relationships with ourselves and with others, trading unhelpful alliances for ones that help us to heal and grow. We can do this with tools that have boosted human resilience in the face of adversity for millennia.

This book will explore three kinds of events that dysregulate our body, mind, and relationships. **Bodily trauma** can include accidents, illness, or injury due to violence, abuse, neglect, and threats of that kind. **Mental and emotional trauma** encompasses events we can't begin to fathom that disrupt our perception of safety in the world. **Traumatic relational events** can include bullying, betrayals, neglect, emotional abuse, racism, and other forms of identity-based bigotry—both macro or micro, explicit and implicit.

Of course, these three types of traumatic events intersect with each other in complex ways. You may have already experienced all three, with compounding effects. When we're ill, people may abandon us. A physical or sexual assault is also a relational betrayal. Marginalized groups are at far higher risk for many traumas, including revictimization when the larger society ignores, belittles, denies, or blames victims for their trauma. That is, when it does not condone or encourage it. All forms of trauma are intersectional in this way.

Our medical model tells us we need to fix trauma, and our culture tells us we need to grow from it, when in fact what we need is to be with ourselves in our pain. And this, itself, is very different from wallowing in pain or pity. This distinction is a key aspect of self-compassion, a central concept in this book. Self-compassion helps us to be okay with the fact that growth and healing happen on different timelines.

How We Grow Through What We Go Through is a buffet of the simplest, best techniques I can offer to encourage post-traumatic growth in our bodies, minds, and hearts. No one of these practices is a cure-all for stress and strife, but most of these should help a little and build up your resilience, like immunity, over time. Try what you like as you read, and come back to what resonates for you, knowing that your tastes and triggers may evolve and change again tomorrow, along with your nervous system. As you explore these practices, adapt them and make them yours. In fact, the more you make them yours and share them, the more they will evolve to help others, too. The more we practice using our inner tools, the more we can all help each other become the kind of people we want to be and want to see.

CHAPTER ONE

Wired for Resilience

Trauma changes everything—from our bodies and brains to our relationships with others and the world. When we experience a severe mental, emotional, or physical injury, we trade perspective, growth, and learning for safety—at least temporarily.

Just about everyone and everything living will experience some kind of trauma at some point, and everyone will react differently and heal differently. More men will experience trauma, but more women will experience complications of trauma and develop PTSD, at least in the reporting. Marginalized groups—people pushed to the edges of an unequal society—are even more likely to experience trauma and the compounding effects of trauma, with less access to healing resources. For some, the body's response may lock in and linger; for others it will fade. But all of us are capable of growth and change, no matter what we have experienced.

Amazingly, research indicates that although 75 percent of us will experience trauma, only 8 to 12 percent will experience PTSD, whereas 60 percent will experience post-traumatic growth (PTG). These are good odds. Even better news: this isn't an either/or situation. PTSD and PTG can happen simultaneously. Neuroscience indicates that growth and pain happen together, just as nearly every spiritual and philosophical tradition teaches.

Let me be clear that trauma and recovery from it are awful, wrenching, slow, unpredictable, and never linear. Nothing can fully soothe our pain all of the time. Tips from friends, therapists, or memes will never "fix" us or make us as we were before. We can't understand each other's pain fully, but we can recognize and witness it in each other—not to fix it or ask it to be fixed, not to try to fix ourselves, but to be with and witness our pain. It is easier to show up and be present for ourselves and others when we have some tools to manage and regulate our trauma responses.

You may be asking yourself if your pain is bad enough to count as trauma. The cliché goes that trauma is a normal reaction to an abnormal event, and it's true. It affects each of us differently, because "normal" and "abnormal" themselves are subjective. Our built-in stress and trauma responses are there to protect us during *and after* a painful experience, and they protect us from future traumas. We end up rewired with sensory triggers for people, places, and things that our nervous systems still believe are dangerous. Over time, when this response becomes automatic and outlives its usefulness, it's labeled as a "disorder," when in fact our nervous systems are just trying to create order out of chaos. In fact, it might be simpler to consider this book as a means of attending to, befriending, resetting, and re-regulating your dysregulated nervous system rather than engaging in a debate about what "counts" as a trauma.

The defenses we fire up under threat are normal and evolutionary. They helped our ancestors and us to survive. The worse or longer the threat, however, the more they rewire our brains. These responses kick into gear when we perceive threat, not necessarily when a threat is there.

Let me say that again: they kick into gear when we *perceive* threat, not necessarily when a threat is there.

With that, let's explore the typical ways we respond to stress and trauma. These are remnants from our ancestors who lived in a far more dangerous world, though it might not seem that way. What was a trauma to our ancestors in times when we were closer to the animals we evolved from? Imagine a lion chasing you. What can you do to survive? I once asked this of an audience in Texas, and there was an actual lion tamer in the audience. Honestly, if she could self-regulate to the point that she could get into a cage with a lion, I don't know why she showed up for my mindfulness class! If *you* are a lion tamer, maybe you can skip ahead.

The Four Fs

There are four ways that we can respond to the attacking lion. Each one of these responses activates our nervous systems for survival in one of two ways, hyperarousal or hypoarousal.

Hyperarousal

1. Fight – Fight off the attacker. This is great if there's a wild animal chasing you, but not great if the "threat" is a traffic jam, a colleague who's getting under your skin, or something that reminds you of your own personal lion. When we fall back on this response, we react with physical or relational aggression or irritability. Sometimes, when we blame ourselves, this flips into aggression toward ourselves in the form of self-harm or risky behavior.

2. Flee – Avoid or evade the attack. This is great if it's a slow lion or you're a fast runner. Not so great if we avoid every situation that's uncomfortable or triggers us. Over time, avoidance can hardwire itself into ongoing anxiety, panic, agoraphobia, and more. Avoidance may also manifest as running toward high-stimulation distractions, addictions, and compulsions.

Hypoarousal

3. Freeze – Hide or camouflage yourself, and try not to be noticed. Perhaps you play dead and give up, waiting for the attack to be over. Hypoarousal may become deliberate avoidance or unconscious dissociation over time. For many from marginalized groups, standing out may feel or be especially dangerous, and this kind of response is truly adaptive for physical, emotional, and even financial safety.

4. Fuck it – Okay, I haven't seen hypoarousal referred to clinically as such! You can also call this "faint or flop." Giving up protects us from lasting trauma in a different way, with "learned helplessness"—a feeling that we have no control or power over our fate. This can wire our brains into depression, a slow giving-up on ourselves and the world, or avoidance strategies like blunting the experience with addiction.

A big enough single, traumatic event or an extensive, long-term trauma rewires our brains to stay in these stress responses all the time. This is the darker side of neuroplasticity. Unless you're a lion tamer, the lion attack is likely a metaphor for something that happened in your life. You likely responded with one or more of these four Fs. That may be how you are still responding to life, long after the lion has gone.

It might sound strange, but our overall arousal level for everyday challenges should be about 60 percent to 80 percent stressed. Above this we're in hyperarousal, with hypoarousal beyond that. It's the right amount of stress within that window of tolerance that helps us grow at the edges. This is the zone where the "magic" happens. That may or may not be "outside your comfort zone," as the meme says, but we have to stay within our safety zone if we want to truly grow. The key to your recovery from trauma is recognizing when you enter your "red" or danger zone and learning how to get back to your safety/growth zone.

Polyvagal theory provides some science behind the magic. Psychologist and researcher Stephen Porges, PhD, and his colleague Deb Dana, LCSW, along with others, have pioneered a new understanding of emotional, social, and physiological regulation based on the functioning of the vagus nerve. This nerve—actually two nerves on either side of the body—is like the information superhighway between the mind and the body. It is the physiology behind a third aspect of our nervous system called the social engagement system, according to Porges. Polyvagal theory has become central to the understanding and treatment of trauma, with more discoveries yet to come.

The reality is, we *need* a stress and fear response. The right amount of fear keeps us safe, and stress can motivate us. If you are in an abusive relationship, it might be safer to be hypoaroused for safety until you can escape. If your military unit is called up, hyperarousal may be exactly what is required. These reactions are warranted and keep you safe. In fact, when a researcher named Arthur Kling removed the amygdala—the brain's alarm system—from a group of captured monkeys and released them back into the wild (this was not the most compassionate research project!) the monkeys were all dead within weeks, having failed to recognize and respond to the dangers around them.

Polyvagal chart

	Freeze or flop	Fight or flight
Arousal Level	Below 30%: Hypoarousal Zone, Dorsal vagal/parasympathetic nervous system activated, Outside the window of tolerance	Above 80%: Hyperarousal Zone, Sympathetic nervous system activated, Outside the window of tolerance
Body	Defensive, shrinking posture, Slow and shallow breathing, Lower blood pressure and heart rate, Reduced immunity, Slow metabolism and high energy food cravings, Cortisol levels lead to physical exhaustion and immobility	Threatening posture, Short, shallow, uneven breathing, Heightened blood pressure and heart rate, Immune system shuts down, Digestive system freezes, Adrenaline, testosterone and cortisol levels lead to aggression and activation toward action
Emotions	Overwhelmed, Giving up, Ashamed, Low confidence, Low motivation Dissociation, Hopelessness	Anxiety, Panic, Fear, Frustration, Rage, Irritation, Panic, Challenged
Perceptions	Scanning for signals to reinforce ways to hide/avoid.	Increase in range of color and sound perception, Neutral social cues perceived as hostile
Brain State and Cognition	Reduced neural activity and reduced cognitive function, Slowed mental processes, Low motivation	Amygdala activated, Outer cortices deactivated, Personalizing, Catastrophizing, Negativity bias, Pessimism, Either/or, rigid thinking, Impulses deactivated
Social	Eye contact and body language shrink, Voice quiet and meek, Avoiding rather than approaching, Isolation, Mistrust, Withdrawal	Eye contact and body language become threatening, Voice agitated and loud, Relational and empathic abilities shut down, Blaming, Scapegoating

	Hurt, not harmed	Attend and befriend
Arousal Level	60-80%: Growth Zone, Nervous system awake and active, Within the window of tolerance	50%: Comfort Zone, Ventral Vagal State, Within the window of tolerance.
Body	Upright confident posture, Breathing deep and slow, 5-6 cycles per minute, Heart rate steady, Immune and digestive systems operating, Oxytocin and testosterone levels boost confidence	Relaxed posture, Breath regulated and slow, Heart slow, circulation flowing evenly, Immune and digestive systems operating optimally, Oxytocin level blocks cortisol, creating room for attachment and feelings of safety
Emotions	Discomfort that does not overwhelm, Engagement, Excitement, Safety, Flow states, High motivation Gratitude, Compassion, Self-compassion, Rising to a challenge	Satisfaction, Grounded, Safe, Warm, Comfortable, Secure, Connected, In control, Not challenged
Perceptions	Accurate and clear, Full range of sensory perception, Finding and seeking meaning, Mindfulness	Largely accurate, Scanning for signs that reinforce safety.
Brain State and Cognition	Outer cortices activated, Well-regulated ,Peak cognitive performance, Critical and nuanced thinking Planning, Impulse control, Setting goals, Active learning, Stretching limits, Curiosity activated	Brain thinking clearly but not overactivated, Clear thinking, Regulated thoughts Unchallenged, Low risk, low reward.
Social	Eyes take in a large middle range of stimuli, Full range of movement, Voice is steady and even, Empathy for and connection to others	Eye movement and senses somewhat reduced, not scanning for danger, Full range of movement, Voice lower and slower Social brain active

Fundamentally, the Four Fs are useful strategies—until they aren't! Like the soldier who scans the highway for the next IED long after arriving home, the cancer survivor who anticipates illness at every ache, or the betrayed spouse who blows up every new relationship as soon as it feels intimate, we may end up hypervigilant after a trauma—scanning for and perceiving danger constantly—because we believe it can keep us safe. For some, even long after a trauma, danger can feel safely familiar, self-harm and addiction might become soothing, disordered eating could create feelings of order, isolation might feel comforting, and connection and compassion could seem overwhelming. And it's not just a mental response: our bodies also stay stuck in these Four Fs. Our responses to trauma help us in the moment and keep us alive, yet they can also interfere with our physical health, mental health, and relationships.

So if these Four Fs are our automatic responses, handed to us by our ancestors and etched onto our DNA for our survival, what can we do to reset ourselves? The answer, thankfully, is *a lot*. Other responses are also built into our DNA, and we can strengthen them through practice. Growing research tells us that it's hard to think our way into a new way of acting and feeling, but we really can act our way into a new way of thinking, feeling, and being. But before we get to that, let's pause here and reflect.

The Four Fs Reflection

- Can you think of a time when you found yourself in one of the Four Fs?

- Are you in one now? If so, what triggered it?

- When you think of a daily stressor—a certain person at work, a financial challenge, a family conflict—does one of the Four Fs match your automatic response?

- How have your stress responses impacted your body, mind, and relationships?

- Which symptoms of the Four Fs do you especially relate to now or in the past?

Let's get back to the lion tamer from Texas. She has learned to override the stress response when most of us would want it to kick in. She's reclaimed her nervous system to the point that when she gets into the cage with the lion, she can stay calm and cope. She can approach, rather than avoid. She can attend to, and even befriend, the lion. She has found a middle way.

This middle path has many names, from spiritual to scientific. It is the state in which we rest and digest, feed and breed, are able to find connection and direction, and do lots of other things that rhyme. We might call it the parasympathetic nervous system, the ventral vagal state, the green zone, the "window of tolerance" as Daniel Siegel calls it, or "in Self" (from Internal Family Systems' theory). Spiritually, we might think of the Buddha's middle path of equanimity, the ability to live "in choice" about how we respond, mindful awareness that leads to compassionate action, or "right effort" (neither over- nor under-exerting for what a situation calls for). Me? I like to call this response Attend and Befriend.

Attend and Befriend

You can get a taste of Attend by holding your body confidently upright with your palms lifted up. Then move your hands to rest over your heart for Befriend. Go back and forth a few times, holding for as long as you like. That's it,— no other special instructions.

Attend

Befriend

As a therapist, I'm kind of obligated to ask a clichéd question: *How does that make you feel?* In fact, I even have it inscribed on a coffee mug. So, how did Attend and Befriend make you feel now—in your body, mind, breath, and heart? In your body, you might notice your breath and heart rates stabilizing and becoming regular and even. In addition, your temperature goes back to baseline as your muscles unclench and relax. The digestive system begins working again, and the immune system gears back up. Blood circulates not just to the vital organs but to your entire body and extremities—no more cold feet. Sugar, fat, and salt are less desirable; you hunger for a range of tastes as your mouth starts salivating again. The parts of your brain that regulate social and sexual systems fire up to connect and care as your empathy and perspective return, so not everyone looks like an enemy. Your brain can suppress impulses, regulate emotions, and focus, and now critical thinking skills return as you see the world as less black and white. Stress hormones that had been clogging your brain wash away and create space for love, trust, and the attachment hormone oxytocin.

The upward spiral continues as you consciously and unconsciously seek out healthy relationships, and they seek you out as a well-regulated human who can reciprocate. Your support network grows to include people who can co-regulate you and inspire you to continue to care for yourself in healthy ways. Your upward spiral could just start with you attending to pets and plants. You have the energy to cook healthfully, to get exercise. Your body feels safe enough to fall asleep and stay asleep through the night.

Now your brain and body are at their best for most tasks, and you can build new connections of support. The window of tolerance is open, and minor stresses roll off you. Feelings of safety return. In your brain, neuroplasticity may even increase, wiring you for more of your brain rewarding your choices with regulated serotonin and happy bursts of dopamine. Your window opens wide to your life. This is the experience of Attend and Befriend.

Fundamentally, this practice and the others that follow are about empowerment, about being able to choose Attend and Befriend over the Four Fs and to override the feeling of powerlessness that is the hallmark of PTSD. On a deep level, a sense of empowerment *protects* us from stress, anger, anxiety, shame, and sadness—even physical pain. True empowerment helps us discern safety from danger, a common confusion in the rewiring that happens due to trauma. This is personal empowerment *within* your own body, mind, and relationships. When we access this way of being, we see the world, friends, and strangers as less threatening, and we're able to be more honest, authentic, and vulnerable in our words and behaviors.

Attend and Befriend is as natural to us as the Four Fs. We don't learn, we don't think, and we don't love unless we feel safe and open enough to Attend and Befriend. With enough practice, we can learn to choose our response to almost any situation we encounter, just like a lion tamer. In the next chapter, we'll learn how the body stores and contains the seeds to heal itself from trauma. In chapter 3, we will cultivate our resilient minds as we learn to stress-proof our brains through positive psychology, mindfulness, and other techniques that undo the "negativity bias."

Negativity Bias: As humans, we're wired to see the glass as half empty rather than half full. If you think evolutionarily, this makes sense: Hear a weird sound in the jungle or glimpse a flash of fur? Better to assume it's a hungry lion than a fluffy little tabbycat. Thus we tend to assume the worst, and in that way we survive and pass on survival-oriented genes that are a little bit pessimistic. Those who assumed the best became lion snacks who didn't have a chance of passing on their optimistic DNA. The positive psychology line is "Your brain is Teflon for the positive, and Velcro for the negative." The ratio is four to one: it takes about four positive experiences to outweigh one negative one.

Last, in chapter 4, we will turn toward resilience in our relationships. This final chapter will help you overcome fear and shame to reach out and build a stronger support network in times of crisis. In addition, you'll learn to more effectively set healthy boundaries in your life—and even online. From there, we can build stronger communities and societies on the other side of adversity, perhaps even create lasting social change.

Thich Nhat Hanh said, "Thinking we should be able to have a life without any suffering is as deluded as thinking we should be able to have a left side without a right side. The same is true of thinking we have a life in which no happiness whatsoever is to be found."

A full life is both/and, not either/or, and too often we assume things are one way or another, when they are in fact multifaceted, multidetermined, and complex. To paraphrase ideas that make the rounds online: You can be grateful and still need more for yourself. You can be resilient and still need rest. You can be fiercely independent and still need and want others. You can be certain and still change your mind. You can be caring and compassionate toward yourself without feeling guilty. You can be kind and generous and still say *no* and set boundaries, knowing that sometimes saying no itself is an act of generosity. You can have done your best in the past, yet since that time, you might have learned new ways of doing things. Finally, other people may have problems and pain, but yours still matter. You can be courageous and still be scared of doing something—yet you can do it anyway.

CHAPTER TWO

Your Resilient Body

In 2013, I was in Helsinki, Finland, leading a mindfulness workshop, when I rather unmindfully checked my phone during the lunch break and found a torrent of messages asking if I was okay. Checking the news, I saw the bloody photos of fearful faces on the Boston streets I'd walked my whole life, at an event I grew up watching a few blocks from my house: The Boston Marathon bombing. Fear struck as my heart clenched, and without consciously being aware, I held my hands on my heart for a moment as my response turned to Befriend. Had I been at the race's finish line, fight, flight, freeze, or flop would have absolutely been the most useful responses, and those Four Fs did save the lives of many people I knew back home. But as I reflected on how I could be most helpful from six thousand miles away, I attended to myself with that simple gesture. I was then able to reach out to my friends and family back home to offer my love and support. That day I showed myself that with enough time and training, we can choose our response to any challenge we face through greater body awareness and empowerment.

In order to heal, we start with the body. If the body does not feel safe, if the nervous system has not been "befriended," as Deb Dana says, growth is more difficult. You, like many of my clients, might reasonably ask: Why would I want to tune in to my body full of pain, sadness, fear, anger, and betrayal? It's true, focusing on the breath can be challenging or triggering for some. Resting in a still body can feel unsettling for many who have experienced trauma. It can be a scary place to begin, but the good news is that you can take back power from your unconscious body again, and that's when healing begins. Long before we find meaning and emotional growth, we can self-regulate our nervous systems through body-based practices. Once we feel empowered in our bodies, our trauma has much less power over us.

As Bruce Lee once paraphrased an ancient Greek philosopher in a meme, "Under duress we do not rise to our expectations but fall to the level of our training." Let's start training.

The Body In Trauma

As we saw in the previous chapter, our bodies respond to trauma and stress—even when we recall it—in ways we seemingly cannot control. The breath and the heart rate are disrupted and biological systems are dysregulated, including appetite and digestion. We crave survival foods like salt, fat, and sugar to give us energy. When we are stressed, we don't crave kale. (Okay, maybe we never crave kale.) Our immune system flickers on and off because energy is conserved for short-term rather than long-term survival. Muscle tension and inflammation become chronic as we adopt rigid, defensive postures and clench our muscles long past when they are helpful. Hot and cold flashes wash over us. We end up sick more often and for longer as the toll from stress wreaks havoc on our immune systems. Worse, this can lead to an infuriating echo when medical professionals dismiss concerns for which they cannot find clear-cut diagnoses, echoing the others who may have dismissed our trauma. This is especially familiar to marginalized folks. To even begin to feel safe in the world, we have to feel safe in our own bodies.

Our bodies are built for occasional, short-term stress responses. The stress response turns on fast, but can take hours to turn off. The more often or longer it gets turned on, the longer before it shuts back down, if ever. This "always-on" response becomes PTSD, whereas an ability to turn off the response prevents PTSD. Embodied practices like Attend and Befriend won't prevent you from getting stressed, but they will help shut down the stress response faster when it's not needed and keep you from permanently rewiring your sytem for dysregulation.

In fact, most recent research on trauma suggests that we cannot begin healing our minds until we feel safe in a body that's healthy, regulated, and trustworthy. Feeling safe and strong in our bodies, we are more likely to perceive new situations as opportunities for growth, rather than threats. We feel "power to" rather than "power over." Engaged and empowered in the world, we scan for new connections, insights, and opportunities, access our creativity, and approach the world from a place of quiet strength.

Your circumstances may make feeling safe in your body a challenge. Perhaps you live with chronic disease or a disability, related or unrelated to your trauma.

Perhaps you've had a sickness or have suffered an injury or assault. Your environment and living situation may be unsafe or feel unsafe. Even in the best of times, physical self-care habits are hard to start and maintain, but you can start simple with some breathing basics that help you self-regulate and manage through challenges. Are these magic bullets? No. Do they all help a little bit? Yes, and they add up, too, little by little. As we learn to become comfortable and empowered in our bodies, we become far more resilient and ready to live safely in our minds and the world.

Your Breath: The Nervous System's Remote Control

You have probably noticed that when you are in one of the Four Fs, your breath becomes dysregulated— slow and shallow, fast and choppy. I even notice this with my own children. Their breathing gets jagged and rough when they're about to get emotional, compared to slow, steady, and smooth when they're immersed in their arts and crafts. Although we adults have bigger bodies, bigger lungs, and sometimes better ways of hiding our emotions, the same holds true for us.

Mood can impact our breath, but the inverse is also true: as we adjust our breath, we can shift our mood. Researchers have used electricity to stimulate the vagus nerve, which appears to be helpful for depression, trauma, and even some autoimmune disorders. The breath can do the same, but more naturally. Our breath is one place where we have conscious control over a part of our autonomic nervous system, unlike our heartbeat or digestion. Breath is like a remote control for our internal alarm system. When the breath is flowing steadily and evenly, everything in our bodies and brains are as well. If you can regulate your breath, you can regulate your body and nervous system, and in turn your brain and your emotions, impulses, and attention. Who doesn't want that superpower?

If the breath is so important, how do we get it right? Most research has landed on a breath rate somewhere between four and six breaths a minute to access your window of tolerance. Depending on your size, that's about five-and-a half-breaths per minute with a five-and-a-half-second inhale and five-and-a-half-second exhale. Interestingly, researchers from Italy found that songs and chants that evolved thousands of miles, years, and cultures apart—such as Hindu mantras and the Latin "Ave Maria,"— bring people into this same optimized, physiological state of breath, heart, blood flow, and more. That same five- to six-second cycle was also found in chants indigenous to Africa, Asia, and the Americas. Later, research on 9/11 survivors found their depression and anxiety significantly reduced when using this same breathing ratio, even without the chants.

A few years back, I had the honor to teach mindfulness and breath work to kids in my old school district. An old friend who'd endured a tumultuous childhood he described as "all chaos, all the time"—even before he was abused by our priest—commented, "Just imagine if we'd been taught mindful breathing when we were in school. How much better we could have managed things." And it's true. I've seen the benefits of learning breathing skills in friends and clients alike.

Using the breath to regulate the nervous system during traumatic experiences or flashbacks is powerful. Like everything in this book, however, breath-work practices are not for everyone. For some people, they might activate *more* anxiety, particularly mindful breathing. Simply watching our breath can be hard to do and is potentially triggering.

However, purposeful, regulated breathing is likely to be more grounding—a more durable anchor—which is why I am offering those practices first. If you do find any of the breathing practices that follow emotionally challenging, you can bring in more grounding by pressing your feet into the ground as you breathe. You can also bring movement into your practice, perhaps by moving your arms. You don't have to stay still. You might also bring imagery to mind, breathing in whatever emotions or qualities you are trying to cultivate and then breathing out what you are letting go of. For instance, you could breathe in confidence and breathe out fear. And, guess what? You can also try one of the dozens of other suggestions and practices throughout this book instead. Skip ahead to the Confident Bodies section on page 33 for body-based practices that aren't based on breathing.

Regulated Breathing

Regulated or intentional breathing is when we deliberately adjust our breathing, slowing and deepening the breath to cultivate the ventral vagal tone of comfort and safety. Short, sharp, irregular breaths that we have when we're anxious are like a 911 call to your sympathetic nervous system, which activates the fight-or-flight response. Meanwhile, shallow, weaker breaths activate the freeze and faint responses. Practicing extended, deeper breaths grabs the remote control away from our trauma and teaches our nervous system to regulate itself. By simply deepening and extending our breath, we activate the vagus nerve to improve communication between all of our organs and brain, thereby boosting health, mental health, and focus. Deliberate, regulated breath work can reduce stress and anxiety, assist with focus and insomnia, cultivate heart rate variability, soothe depression, and even boost immune system function.

> **Heart Rate Variability** (HRV) is a measure of the rhythms of the space between heartbeats. HRV tracks directly to the breath rate. When dysregulated, HRV may contribute to heart disease, cancer, depression, anxiety, and PTSD. Low HRV—a lack of change in our heart's rhythm—corresponds to a lack of nervous system balance and difficulty in meeting the moment. High HRV corresponds to balance between the parasympathetic and sympathetic nervous systems and the ability to be in the right state to meet the moment.

Adjusting your breath speed, depth, and ratio turns down the volume on the emotional response and can even change the channel on your mood. In fact, researchers find you can track your breathing rate and ratio to get familiar with how you breathe when you are angry or calm, sad or joyful, frustrated or excited, or even facing addictive urges. You can then actually alter your mood by following a chosen breath pattern. Different breath ratios even regulate our social system, helping us to engage rather than withdraw.

The Remote Control: Four Ways to Regulate Your Breath

There are a few simple ways to reset your breath that you may already do without realizing it. Those of us who don't have the patience to meditate may be too self-conscious to go to a yoga class or are too skeptical to believe in prayer. However, we can still access the documented benefits of all three by regulating our breath. You can access simple breath regulation from anywhere.

1. Stretch the Breath

Not only do the lungs have nerves that connect to the nervous system, there are also different nerve endings at the bottom and the top of our lungs. Those at the bottom send a signal to relax and shut down the fight-or-flight response. Taking a deep breath metaphorically hits a reset button in our lungs and nervous system, allowing us to relax. I recommend starting with an inhale through the nose and then gently extending and stretching out the exhale from the mouth. It should take you about five seconds to breathe out and another five or so seconds to breathe in again. This way, you'll have a breath rate of about five breaths per minute.

2. Hands on Head

Fleet Maull, who has taught trauma-sensitive mindfulness in prisons, where he spent two decades himself, recommends simply putting your hands behind your head and leaning back as you breathe. Without much effort, this posture stretches the vagus nerve; deepens, slows, and regulates your breath; and even changes your body chemistry. Try it now and see what you notice. Many of us already stretch our bodies like this in an act of unconscious self-regulation.

3. A Silent Sigh

The other thing many of us do spontaneously a few dozen times a day is sighing to release stress and frustration. Think about it: a sigh is merely a long, stretched-out, even exhalation that we almost always use to reset ourselves. The sound may also relax our muscles through vibration, like a chant, but a silent sigh works as well. Any time you think of it, you might take a deep breath in and let it out in a silent sigh. How does it make you feel?

4. Counting Breaths

A more deliberate breathing technique is to count along with the breath. I like the 7-11 Breath, which is easy to remember. Simply inhale while counting to seven, and exhale while counting to eleven. (Try it whenever you drive past a 7-Eleven store.) A similar variation, often recommended for sleep, is the Triangle Breath, or 4-7-8 Breath: inhaling for four counts, holding for seven, and exhaling for eight counts. The Four Square Breath, or Box Breath, is another option: inhale as you count to four, hold your breath in for four counts, exhale for four counts, and hold your breath out for four. Then repeat.

Consciously regulating your breath often feels awkward at first and might take some practice. The point is to find a way to regulate your nervous system with the breath in a way that feels comfortable for you. The breath can then become responsive to something difficult or preventive as we approach challenging or triggering situations.

Alan had grown up with a father whose anger was explosive and seemed to come out of nowhere, and he was working incredibly hard not to follow in his father's footsteps. Mindful breathing, just watching his breath, was a step too far for Alan; his mind would wander and he found it frustrating. But regulated breathing helped him settle quickly when he got triggered. It felt like a natural match with some breath work he'd done as a hockey goalie back in high school—another time in his life when he had a lot flying at him and needed to keep his cool. He practiced the 7–11 Breath at red lights in traffic when he frequently lost his cool or when sitting in the driveway before he walked into the house to see his wife and family, who often triggered him in similar ways as his father. If Alan ever felt ungrounded by the breath, he would keep his eyes open, move his arms up a bit, or press his feet into the ground as he breathed. Like many people, it felt too unanchored for Alan to just watch the breath, so deliberately counting breaths was a way for him to get some objective distance. If you do want to try mindful breath awareness, you might also use some visualization to help. As a lifelong beach bum, I find it helpful to visualize and feel the breath like waves, as I do in the following practice.

Ocean-Wave Breathing

Allow yourself in this practice to really savor and enjoy the breath as it simply washes over you and through you, massaging and even caressing you inside and out.

- Close, soften, or lower your eyes, and simply become aware of your breath.

- Pay particular attention to the sounds and sensations of the breath, which remind you that you are breathing.

- Tune in to your breath's gentle whooshing sound, listening as if your breath is waves lapping at the shore. Feel the gentle rise and fall of ocean waves.

- As you connect with the breath, notice the ways that some breaths, like some waves, are smoother or rougher, longer or shorter.

- Like waves, breaths just keep coming, one after the next, washing away both wanted and unwanted thoughts, emotions, and memories, breath by breath.

Mindful breathing can inform regulated breathing. As you continue to watch and listen to your breath, eventually you will get to know how the patterns of breath are influenced by your mood, just as the tides are influenced by the moon. And better yet, you can adjust the flow of your breath and allow yourself to practice making small shifts to your own breath.

Try watching your breath over the course of your day, noticing the breath ratio and rhythm in different moods, different places, and different situations. You can watch it like the waves of the ocean, count breaths, or just enjoy your breath with all of your senses. As you get to know your breath, try shifting the ratios or using different regulated-breath practices like the 7–11 Breath or Triangle Breath. Even a simple long sigh or stretch regulates and resets the nervous system. You are the one in control.

Confident Bodies

One of my first jobs as a research assistant was watching videotapes of people in therapy. With practice, we researchers could watch the videos on mute and almost diagnose people based on their body language alone. How would you describe someone overcome by depression, trauma, or shame? Every time I ask this at one of my workshops, I hear the same things: "Sleeping on the couch at weird hours, if they sleep at all." "Eating too much, or not at all." "Staring at a screen all day." "Isolating and never leaving the house or seeing people." "Not showering or even getting out of pajamas." Sometimes people even slump over to demonstrate a freeze/faint posture. Now, describe yourself when the state of your world catches up with you—say, at the start of the pandemic. Notice any similarities?

Our mental health impacts our bodies and behavior, but the reverse is also true. In fact, all the time we spend hunched over screens alters our breath patterns and likely impacts our mood and confidence, even making us less assertive, according to the science. Today's psychotherapists recognize that even if we become paralyzed by trying to think ourselves into a new way of acting, we can act our way into a new way of thinking and feeling. Just as the breath changes with our mood—and vice versa—so too our bodies change in relation to how we feel, *and* we can change how we feel by changing our bodies. It's the inverse of the depression that circumstances like the shame of trauma or chronic illness can force us into. Trauma is about feeling powerless. The more we can develop an internal locus of control, the better we fare in future stressful and traumatic situations or crises.

Getting comfortable in your body—and better yet empowered in it—is the first step toward healing and feeling empowered in your life. You might start with simple stretching. The health and mental benefits of yoga are vast and well researched for depression, mindfulness, and more. If you are still actively struggling with trauma reactions, finding trauma-informed yoga teachers could be critical for keeping you in your safety zone.

Positive psychologist and researcher Emma Seppälä studied how yoga affected war veterans, and she found reductions in hypervigilance, startle response, breath rates, and regulation months after the yoga class ended. In addition, the yoga-practicing vets experienced fewer anxiety symptoms such as nightmares and flashbacks. The more expansive yoga postures are usually the most empowering—especially chest-opening postures that deepen the breath, such as Cobra Pose, Upward-Facing Dog, and the like. But you don't have to practice yoga to experience the power of changing your posture to change your mood. Dr. Amy Cuddy is famous for discovering that the Wonder Woman posture—standing up straight with your hands on your hips—can shift your body chemistry. Her book, *Presence: Bringing Your Boldest Self to Your Biggest Challenges*, is based on her successful TED Talk about "power postures," and it explores the mind-body connection more deeply. Further investigation by her research team found even more compelling evidence to back up the healing effects of how we inhabit our bodies.

One of my clients, Sarah, had suffered a violent assault as a Peace Corps volunteer. She first entered my office with her eyes downcast because she was afraid of making eye contact and of being noticed. Her hands covered her neck to protect her jugular veins, though it had been months since the assault. I recommended that she try Dr. Cuddy's power postures. "Once I starting inhabiting my body fully and confidently," Sarah reported, "the pain from the injuries subsided, or at least it didn't bother me the same way it had before. It no longer kept me from doing what I wanted to do. I believed it might happen, because I liked the science from Amy Cuddy's TED talk, and then I started to believe that body postures like the Wonder Woman stance would help me to tolerate my fear and move on from the shame and self-blame I felt, too. And it did."

Picture an athlete after scoring a goal, arms raised high in victory. This physical attitude, like the Wonder Woman posture or even sitting upright, appears to shift our body chemistry. Testosterone is released, and the stress hormone cortisol is curtailed in these poses. Confidence and leadership tend to correlate with high testosterone and low cortisol. Though testosterone is often misunderstood as an aggression hormone, the reality is that it's linked to assertiveness, status, and leadership in both men and women. It also correlates with the idea of empowerment or "self-leadership," which is described as an ideal state by Richard C. Schwartz, the creator of Internal Family Systems therapy. Only when testosterone is paired with damaging cortisol does it seem to lead to aggression and the fight-or-flight response. When both are elevated, we become toxic to ourselves and others.

Like my client, you can use power postures to regulate and reduce cortisol, regulate your nervous system, and regain your brain and best self. This empowerment comes from the right balance of these neurotransmitters to create self-regulation with self-confidence. The key is how you inhabit your own body.

Healthy embodiment, which is expansive like the athlete with his arms raised, is a protective factor. When we're traumatized, however, we take up less physical and interpersonal space and even use less brain space. Our perspective is inhibited; by looking down in shame, we literally see less of the world. Inhibition assumes that anything new is a threat, as opposed to a neutral or even potential opportunity. This anxiety only begets more anxiety, and we are farther and farther away from our true selves. Confidently inhabiting our bodies can help us lead our fullest lives out to the edges of our safety zone, which is where we grow. Ask yourself: How do I typically inhabit my body? How far do I stretch it physically? How much space do I occupy? Does it feel safe to do so? What messages have you received about taking up space? What is my body language communicating to the world and, more importantly, what is it communicating to others? Notice your voice and posture through the day in different settings, interactions, and activities. Add a power posture or two into a safe time and place in your day and see if there's a shift internally. If it makes sense, add these postures at times you're with others. Even internally visualizing ourselves in a confident posture can make a difference in how we feel.

Our elders were onto something when they told us to stand up straight, shoulders back, third button out. If you are physically limited, permanently or temporarily, make these empowering postures in your imagination. Research finds that it's almost as good.

Power Postures

Notice your posture, breath, and even your voice throughout the day. What do they communicate to you and to others? Consider what a shame or trauma posture looks and feels like and how that compares to a confident dance gesture, a performance bow, an expansive Sun Salutation, bench-pressing free weights, crossing the finish line with your arms stretched triumphantly, hitting a home run, or acing a tennis ball.

One of my clients who had been mercilessly bullied and hazed as a teenager found she could shift her mood when she stood and walked with her head high. People treated her differently: new kinds of people approached her, and others avoided her. She would even practice "pendulating" from inhibited to expansive postures to cultivate confidence and creativity.

Adopting more powerful postures helps us take more calculated risks by putting ourselves out there in healthy ways. For instance, holding a power posture, even while you're getting criticized, can help those criticisms roll off your back. And holding your head high in the face of life's challenges really helps.

Tone of voice also shifts with posture. When our posture is confident, even our word choice becomes more assertive, and that changes how people respond to us. When we breathe a "happy" breath and sit in a confident posture, we tend to have happier memories and better abstract thinking. When sitting, standing, or walking in a slumped posture, we tend to notice the negative, which reinforces a negative outlook. Try it and see for yourself!

As we saw with the Attend and Befriend practice, we can also offer ourselves powerful gestures of compassion to regulate our trauma responses. Researcher and writer Dacher Keltner reminds us that a warm, consensual touch from a friend, a pet, or even ourselves is a message of safety and trust that helps us connect with others, soothes our nervous systems, and teaches us to tolerate vulnerability. Christopher Germer and Kristin Neff, who developed the Mindful Self-Compassion Program, recommend the gentle warmth and pressure of your hand on any place you feel tension or emotion, or gently cradling and supporting your own head in a moment of stress.

Supportive Touch

During a stressful moment, let yourself enjoy a few relaxing breaths, followed by placing one or both hands over your heart as we did earlier in the book. Experience this gentle touch from the outside, as you offer it, and from the inside where it lands, offers comfort, and perhaps even spreads outward. If this triggers self-consciousness, you might give yourself a gentle hug, hold your hands or face, or just feel your hands resting in each other or on your lap. Take a moment to savor these sensations, perhaps even feeling the warmth and affection spread from your hands through the rest of your body. This is also an excellent practice for sleep.

You might even go a step farther and offer yourself a "butterfly hug" variation, developed to soothe trauma. Begin by giving yourself a hug across your shoulders, then raise your arms and gently alternate affectionate tapping with your hands on each shoulder or offering yourself a gentle caress as you regulate your breath. Touching this way creates a soothing sensation and evokes bilateral stimulation.

Bilateral stimulation is when we stimulate both hemispheres of the brain at the same time. We do this every time we walk, run, swim, bike, or perform any other activity that engages both sides of our body simultaneously. Intentional bilateral stimulation via tapping on both sides of the body is used in trauma therapies such as Brainspotting and EMDR (Eye Movement Desensitization Reprocessing).

Move a Muscle, Change a Thought: Embodied Movement

I once asked a colleague who is a well-known neuroscientist what she considered the best thing to do for brain health. "That's easy," she replied. "Exercise."

"But what *kind* of exercise?" I asked. "Meditation, crossword puzzles, sudoku, learning a language?"

No, no, no!" She cut me off brusquely. "The best thing you can do for brain health is physical exercise. Move your body!"

The more I investigated, the more science confirmed her words. Light exercise, even a twenty-minute walk a few times a week if you can, is as good for mild to moderate depression as many medications. Anxiety and focus also improve after exercise, as does sleep. In fact, yoga postures were likely developed to aid in focus during longer meditations and learning—not for physical fitness or feats of flexibility.

We've all heard a story of someone who ran a marathon after beating cancer. One of my clients hiked the Himalayas after a divorce, and I treated a student who bulked up their body after an assault to defend themself from that ever happening again. That's not most of us, and it doesn't have to be. (I confess that the Himalayas, though beautiful, were also pretty lonely when I hiked them in my twenties!) Building physical strength can give us a new trust in our bodies that we might feel have been betrayed or have betrayed us. Exercise and mobility goals, however small, give us something to work toward and create a sense of purpose. Moreover, many of us may have to deal with limited mobility, in which case I hope there are plenty of other approaches besides movement that bring your body peace.

Contemplative movement, be it ritual dance, sport, martial arts, or something else, exists in every culture. Trauma researcher Peter A. Levine suggests that deliberately shaking the body, like animals in nature after a fight, can shake off the stress response—dancing and rocking can serve this purpose as well. Mindful and compassionate walking is one of many simple ways to get started with moving and inhabiting your body in a safe way. By slowing down, we can more fully embody our experience, both internally and in our surroundings. So-called "walking meditation" is also a powerful reminder that mindfulness is not a still, solitary, indoor activity but one that can be done in embodied movement.

In fact, research finds that walking practice is often what people describe as their favorite practice after taking a mindfulness or self-compassion course, and the one they are most likely to continue to practice. Here are a few ways to bring more awareness into walking and to make it a potent tool for mental wellness.

Seven Walking Practices

Walking is something many of us practice daily, and like breathing it's usually something we do without much thought. It's a workout for both your body and the emotion-regulating parts of your brain all at the same time. Most of the following practices can be done anywhere—in a park or a parking lot. If walking is not your thing, or if your mobility is limited, know that you can benefit from applying mindful attention to any form of movement. Many veterans and others with mobility issues apply and adapt these concepts to using their chairs or other assistive devices.

1. Basic Walking Meditation

Begin by simply noticing yourself walking as you walk, bringing attention to body sensations and perhaps to the soles of your feet across different surfaces.

To break out of the autopilot we are often in, you might ask yourself, *How do I know I am walking*? and then check in with your senses. Notice not just what your legs are doing but also your arms, torso, spine, and head as you walk. You might be able to detect subtle shifts in your pulse, body temperature, or breathing rate before, during, and after you begin moving. You can also focus on the gentle rocking motion of your weight shifting.

Sometimes in sitting meditation, we use our breath as our anchor and focus on the point between the in-breath and the out-breath when there's a moment of stillness. Likewise, in walking practice we can notice the points of stillness where the right step becomes the left step and the left step becomes the right step.

There's no right way to do this, so just let yourself explore and see what, if anything, resonates for you as you embody each step.

2. Walking with Words

Sometimes simple, mindful walking is a challenge for our agitated minds. You may feel bored or self-conscious. If that's the case, count in rhythm with your steps. Whenever your mind wanders off and you lose count, simply notice where your mind has wandered and then return to the count, starting at one. The key, of course, is to do this without judging yourself or your wandering mind so harshly. The practice, as they say, is in coming back.

It may also help to have something to say along with the movements. You can, for example, say thank you and send gratitude or compassion to your feet and body as you move—another mindful, self-compassion practice. This might help if you have experienced a bodily betrayal. You could also quietly or internally repeat reminder phrases to yourself. You might enjoy repeating the following phrases suggested by Thich Nhat Hanh with each step:

I have arrived,
I am home,
In the here,
In the now.

Once I heard a friend speak some other wonderful phrases for each footstep:

Nowhere to go.
Nothing to do.
No one to be.

One of my workshop participants recommended that we leave something behind with each footstep, like a legacy:

With each step, I move toward what I want to become and away from what and where I was.

Experiment with any or all of these as you walk, or come up with your own phrases that resonate for you next time you take a walk. If you can get outside into nature, so much the better, as we discuss next.

3. Sensory Forest Walking

Many of us have experienced the healing power of nature—from mountains to beaches—to soothe our most turbulent emotions. The states of wonder and awe are proven to boost our mood and emotional resilience, and we're wired to feel them when we're among nature's naturally repeating fractal shapes: tree branches, leaf veins, seashells, flowers, cloud formations, and coastlines. In short, time in nature has its benefits, and so does exercise. So why not combine them and double the effect?

The Japanese walking meditation practice of forest bathing emphasizes our five senses, reliably bringing us into the present moment. Our minds might race to horror stories of the future or past, but our senses ground us. As we come into the here and now, we can savor the precious moments we can devote to moving in the outdoors and appreciating all that is around us. The next time you find yourself in the company of trees, you might give it a try:

- First, walk while keeping your eyes still and watching the view change as shapes and objects shift in and out of your line of vision. Notice colors and shades of colors. Notice shapes repeating themselves in nature's fractal patterns. Notice the shapes of the spaces between everything.

- Next, let your eyes go where they will, and focus your attention only on the soles of your feet, being aware of different sensations such as changes in the walking surface and how your steps adapt to it. Notice also the following sensations: your skin against your clothing, the temperature and texture of the air, the sun against your skin.

- Shift your awareness to sounds: your own footsteps, the changing sounds around you as you move, the trees whispering, the river's babbling, the ocean sighing, and whatever else comes to your attention.

- Now focus on scents and tastes in the air, paying attention to how they change depending on where you are. Notice your emotional reactions to what you smell as you breathe in the gift of oxygen from the trees, then exhale your offering of CO_2, which sustains them in our interdependence.

- Finally, and for the remainder of your walkabout, consider focusing on the pleasant aspects of what you encounter on your walk—as this, too, has been shown to shift mood and outlook.

Shinrin-yoku, the practice known as "forest bathing," was developed by Japanese doctors in the 1980s. In fact, the Japanese government has invested millions in research and established hundreds of forest-therapy centers, which are now spreading around the world. Spending time in the woods seems to lower heart rate, improve cognition, and boost immune response. Just living closer to forests appears to correlate with lower rates of cancer and better health overall.

Phytoncides, chemicals released by plants, seem to lower stress hormones, anxiety, aggression, and depression, and they appear to regulate pain and immune function, including boosting the immune system's "natural killer cells" for as long as a week after a walk in the woods.

Spending time in nature can boost alpha waves, activate serotonin, and regulate anxiety and aggression. Vitamin D, which we get from the sun, boosts health and regulates mood; exposure to sunshine also improves melatonin levels, which regulate our sleep.

One study showed that patients in hospital rooms that overlooked trees healed faster, with less pain medication and fewer postsurgical complications. Even a photograph of nature correlated with lower cortisol, better immune function, and fewer requests for pain medication. There's evidence that having plants in offices boosts focus, productivity, and well-being by 47 percent, while also improving our mood. Plants in homes appear to extend the lives of the elderly, while the sight of fresh flowers lifts our spirits and focus.

4. Embodied Awareness Walking

It's fun to make up your own walking meditation practices. One I've been playing with recently is walking as I turn my awareness on parts of the body, fully feeling them and offering them gratitude, almost like a body scan in motion.

- As you walk, begin by resting your awareness on your feet, bringing attention to the soles of your feet.

- After about twenty steps, shift your awareness to your ankles and calves, offering them some thanks.

- After a few minutes with your attention there, rest some grateful attention on the bending of your knees.

- Next, focus awareness on the sensations and movement of your hips.

- After some time focused on the hips, shift awareness to your hands and arms—how they naturally fall to your sides or how they swing as you walk. Enjoy and appreciate their strength.

- You might then shift to awareness of the sensations in your torso, including your heart and lungs, noticing how they've changed.

- After a few moments of attention in your torso, turn it to your neck and shoulders.

- Finally, notice your head as it shifts and moves slightly up and down with each footstep.

- Continue to scan your body as you walk, noting how sensations change over the course of your walk.

5. Appreciative Walking

Numerous studies have found that appreciating our surroundings as we walk tends to have a lasting effect on our mood long after we stop moving, similar to the way other gratitude practices work. This research is the inspiration for another walking practice: simply noticing beauty in the world around us as we walk.

On your walk, make a regular practice of noticing at least one positive thing along the way: something beautiful, something funny, or an act of kindness. What captures your attention? A particularly beautiful shaft of light, a house or car painted in your favorite color, the scent of a tree in bloom? You might note these to yourself in a journal, snap a photo, or tell the story of your walk to someone else.

If you take the same route each day, choose to focus on the changes you encounter. Day by day, watch as the seasons gradually shift. How do the sights, sensations, smells, and sounds change? What one new thing each day on your walk do you find? How about at different times of day, or how weekends compare to weekdays?

6. Walking "As If"

How we walk and move changes how empowered we feel, and that empowerment affects how we're perceived by the world. Amy Cuddy's research on body postures shows that when we "walk small," which we may do to avoid being targeted, we feel worse than when we "walk tall" and signal our confidence to ourselves and the world. What does walking tall mean? Longer strides, swinging arms, larger hand and arm movements. We take up our rightful space in the world, we reclaim it from wherever trauma took it, and sometimes we take even a little more space than we previously owned.

You can explore your emotions by noticing how they affect your walking, what you observe on your walk, and vice versa. How does your movement, what you see, or how you respond shift when you're happy or sad, calm or anxious, frustrated or relaxed? How does the way you walk and what you notice affect how you feel? You can even do this on purpose. Try walking like you are fearful or anxious. Then walk as if you are loaded down by shame, feel distracted, or are annoyed. After that, try walking confidently or happily—whatever that means to you. Perhaps you could pretend you are an official from Monty Python's Ministry of Silly Walks, as recommended by pediatrician Jan Chozen Bays, who works with abused children. Then shift back into your regular rhythm and gait, if you can still find it. How do you feel?

How you hold your body both in stillness and in motion affects your perception, self-perception, and much more. If you can act your way into a new way of thinking, it follows that you can move your way into a new way of feeling.

7. Walking for Self-Discovery

When trauma inhibits us and we shrink from our surroundings, we can try to lean into it by getting curious about the world and our emotional reactions to it. Try this as you walk. What do you notice in yourself as someone nears your personal space? As you pass a particular landmark? This might raise discreet feelings of self-consciousness as you pass others, or a slight pleasure when you step into sunshine, followed by the slightest dread as a small hill approaches. People, places, sounds, and even times of day might provoke the subtlest of reactions. Reflect on all of these, noticing where on the spectrum of moods and emotions your regular pace of walking takes you.

Integrating mindfulness into movement has the added benefit of combining mental with physical exercise. In addition to giving our brains a good workout with mindfulness, we're also doing something great for our physical and mental health by moving. Plus, getting playful can shake off self-consciousness and enhance cognitive flexibility. Trauma can rob us of joy, but playfulness brings it back, boosting creativity and our connection with friends, family, and even strangers.

Feeding Our Resilience

Think back to the stress response: if you're being chased by a lion, what kinds of foods might you be craving, besides maybe lion jerky? Probably a balance of salts, fats, sweets, and other foods that offer a caloric blast to provide energy you'll need to fight or flee the lion. I don't think any of my cave-dwelling ancestors who escaped the lion and passed on their genes to me were craving kale in that moment. Or, perhaps, ever.

Nor for that matter, did our noble ancestors take forty minutes to mindfully eat a raisin before hitting the Serengeti to search for food. I can still remember the raisin from that first Mindfulness-Based Stress Reduction class I took more than half a lifetime ago. I was only twenty years old and spent twenty-five minutes mindfully masticating the single little raisin doled out to us with all of the attention and wonder in my being. From that first awe-inspiring taste onward, I was hooked on exploring mindfulness. I walked out of the class with the zeal of the newly converted, promising myself I would eat every meal like I ate that raisin. Fast-forward just a few hours, and I was cramming pizza down my throat while watching reruns of *The Simpsons* on my parents' basement TV. After that I limited my mindful eating practice to a once-a-month sushi meal eaten in silence with no distractions.

As the years slipped past, prioritizing a formal mindful meal slipped away. Once I had kids, it became nigh impossible. As I more deeply explored "informal" mindfulness, I started to get it. With some self-compassion, we can bring "more mindfulness" to eating, as opposed to perfect formality on one hand or completely mindless eating on the other. For our purposes here, taking a self-compassionate approach to eating can help us get the nutrition we need for our brain health. This in turn grants more resilience in the face of stress. And speaking of self-compassion, the next time you crave a cookie, remember that it might just be your body's way of trying to escape that lion.

Many of us have a complicated relationship to food and eating, after receiving deeply mixed cultural messages from society or our families about food and our bodies. Add stress and trauma, and even long after the stress has passed, our appetites and metabolism can remain significantly disrupted and dysregulated. For others, certain foods might trigger unwanted emotions. For those struggling with medical issues, our appetites may be significantly impacted, or strict diets imposed by doctors might make us feel even more disempowered in our bodies and choices.

The following Mindful Eating Chart offers six simple guidelines for caring more deeply for your body and mind, as well as ways to find that balance between mindless eating and self-compassionate, (more) mindful eating. Remember, you don't have to eat perfectly—just consider these suggestions as inspiration for how to approach food. Eating well gives your body and brain the energy and strength needed to more effectively regulate your nervous system and emotions—and thereby help you feel more empowered over choices in your life.

Slowing down is one of the best ways to get the mind and body to communicate about what we really need—a system that may be broken by trauma. The body actually sends its satiation signal about twenty minutes after the brain does, which is why we often unconsciously overeat. So if you slow down even a little bit, you can give your body a chance to catch up to your brain and then eat only what you need.

Simple ways to slow down might include paying attention to some of your grandmother's manners, such as sitting down to eat, chewing each bite twenty-five times, and setting down your fork between bites. All those "old-fashioned" manners may not be not as pointless as they seem. Consuming smaller portions and checking in between bites also slows down eating so that you can be more mindful. Ask yourself: Are you eating past fullness and ignoring your body's signals, or do you slow down when you eat and stop when your body says it's full?

Mindless versus Mindful Eating

Mindless Eating	(More) Mindful Eating
Eating past fullness and ignoring the body's signals that it's full	Listening to your body and stopping when you're full
Eating when emotions tell us to eat (e.g., sad, anxious, lonely)	Eating when our bodies tell us to eat (e.g., stomach is growling, energy is low)
Eating at random times and places or missing meals	Eating intentionally and with predictable routines and places
Eating foods that are just emotionally comforting	Eating a range of foods, including those that are nutritionally healthy
Eating and multitasking	When eating, you don't do anything but eat
Considering a meal an end product	Considering where your food comes from

What are some other ways you can slow down while eating and listen more deeply to your body's signals?

If our bodies have betrayed us or been betrayed, we often listen first to our minds—but like many mind-body approaches, it might more wise to tune in to our bodies first. Rather than just eating when we get emotional signals—which may be different for each of us—we can listen to our bodies. Is your stomach growling, your energy low, or do you feel a little lightheaded? Too often, emotions guide our choices, and although emotions can be useful, we could tune in to our bodies. True mindful eating for resilience involves listening deeply to our body's signals of hunger. To be sure, make a couple of inquiries:

Am I responding to an emotional want or responding to a physical need?

What are my body's hunger signals, and what are my emotional hunger triggers?

Other common, mindless ways to eat include wandering around looking through cabinets and eating at random times and places, rather than eating with some intention. These might be leftover habits from the chaos of a difficult time in your life or times you used food to self-soothe. This does not mean you have to be perfect now, but *some* intention regarding meals and snacks can help.

Eating at specific times and in specific places slows us down and helps us develop healthy environmental cues about what and how much to eat. Do you really want to strengthen the habit of eating every time you get in the car or switch on the TV? We all snack, but our physical and mental health are aided by routines. In addition, our bodies know when to sleep, based in part on our meal times. (That's a pro tip from a former frequent flyer.) This means we should try to establish a consistent time to sit down at a table and eat with utensils from a plate or bowl rather than a takeout container. This reminds us that eating can be a special—even sacred—act of self-care.

It may help to eat with others. Not only are you sharing and getting some healthy connection, you're also more likely to slow down and enjoy the food and conversation more. What's more, we take cues from our dinner partners, which helps keep us from over- or under-eating out of emotion. And when you plan a meal, no matter how vague, you're also more likely to eat the amount your body needs in that moment than you are to undereat or overindulge later.

When we put our food out of sight in cabinets and the fridge, we're less likely to be cued to eat too much. If you, like me, forget to eat when stressed, you might do the opposite. When you stick with eating at the table, you are also less likely to multitask. And, of course, follow the advice to shop with a list and not when you're hungry or emotional. Remember that when we're stressed, eating can be an afterthought. It's easier to get takeout or open a bag of chips when we're wiped out than it is to prepare a healthy lunch. Of course, some degree of relying on convenience food is fine so long as we aim to bring more awareness and intention to eating. It can help to reflect on these questions:

Are you eating randomly or following at least some sort of routine?

Do you have a sense of when you are eating?

Although I don't want to endorse a specific diet, I have always found journalist Michael Pollan's "food rules" to be a useful guide: don't eat foods your grandparents would not recognize, stay away from processed foods with too many ingredients or ones you can't pronounce, shop the perimeter of the grocery store, eat until you're almost—but not quite—full, and keep mealtime sacred and social when possible.

One reason the mindful raisin-eating exercise works is that when we slow down and eat healthy foods, we often enjoy them more than the story we tell ourselves about healthy foods. As we practice eating a greater variety of nutritious foods, we are less inclined to binge on comfort foods and more inclined to enjoy healthy foods, ultimately finding them emotionally and physically satisfying.

Classic advice is to not shop when hungry and to avoid the cookie aisle, but beware the psychological effect known as "moral licensing." Research finds that if you convince yourself that you're being "good" when you buy kale, you're more likely to justify heading to the alcohol or ice cream section of the grocery store than when you don't. We seem to think that our karma will balance out and we can "spend" it on more junk food. Remember, this isn't about being perfect; it's about finding balance.

When you're preparing or eating foods, notice:

Are you eating foods that are emotionally comforting or foods that are also nutritionally healthy?

Are you finding a balance between healthy foods and those that are just comfort foods?

Food connects us to others. When we pause to consider all of the people involved in a meal that arrives on our plates—from loved ones who prepared it (including you), to those who stocked the shelves, to the dock workers and truck drivers in the supply chain, to those who planted and harvested the raw ingredients, and to those who supported all these people—it is almost impossible not to feel both grateful and interconnected. In addition to the network of people involved, we can reflect on the cultural traditions that brought us our cuisine, the recipes generously shared by friends or brought from a distant place and time to be handed down in the family, often carried alongside stories of both resistance and resilience. This contemplation has been personally healing. It was while mindfully eating one day that I realized my habits connected me with the violence of the drug trade. This insight played an enormous role in waking me up from addiction and moving past it.

Thich Nhat Hanh reminds us to "drink our cloud" as we drink our tea, ever mindful of the water, soil, and other elements that were part of its creation. You, too, can be mindful of these as you sit down to eat. You can offer thanks to the animals and ecosystems that were sacrificed for your meals.

As you consider everything that went into the meal and everyone who contributed to bringing it to your table, it becomes almost effortless to experience and express gratitude to all of the people and elements who gave their time and effort—and at times their lives—to sustain us. With a little more mindful awareness, we may begin to make wiser choices about sustainability and health in our food, not just for us but for the whole planet, making us all more resilient as a result.

Contemplate:

Where does your food come from?

How does your meal connect you to your family, your community, the larger culture, the world?

I saw a meme a few years back that said "There's a guy at this coffee shop, sitting at a table, not on a phone, not on a laptop, just drinking his coffee. Like a psychopath." It's so rare that we see this, but if you give it a try, I guarantee the rest of your day will go differently.

Multitasking and eating is, well, a recipe for ignoring the body's needs and wants. We've all had the experience of going into a movie with a bag full of popcorn, and before the trailers are over, we are wondering who ate all the popcorn. When we are distracted, it becomes harder to listen to our body's signals about food and other needs. With your next meal, try "single-tasking" and just eating, with no screens or distractions. Simply enjoy the company and conversation you are sharing.

You'll also know you're eating more mindfully because you'll feel better physically and emotionally before, during, and after eating. Or maybe you can relate to my patient, who is also a comedian, who once joked to me that "eating healthy feels great because you get to feel smug and superior to everyone else who doesn't eat healthy." I'm not sure whether that's the best reason, but hey, whatever gets you to self-care.

Consider:

What activities do you often combine with eating?

What happens when you "just eat?"

Sleep Is Medicine

Okay, you probably already get it that sleep is good and, yes, it's far easier said than done during or after a trauma. Stress and trauma convince our bodies that becoming vulnerable enough to sleep is a danger, so we stay on extra-high alert, which makes it hard to fall asleep and stay asleep. For some, the fear of nightmares makes sleep even more frightening, and the nervous system guards against that, too.

A few things can help. For one, eating regularly and exercising both cue our bodies to sleep on a schedule, and vice versa, so routines become important. Your life doesn't have to take on a rigid structure, especially when you're in crisis, but familiar routines and rhythms have been shown to ease our anxiety about what comes next, open up more brain bandwidth for the emotional work we're doing, and give us things to look forward to. So-called "sleep hygiene" practices such as getting up and going to bed at approximately the same times help, too. Other sleep facilitators include a cool, dark room; soothing, safety-inducing sounds or a white-noise machine; and turning off screens an hour or so before bedtime.

Research confirms what we all know for ourselves: not sleeping makes us feel worse. Sleep impacts our physical immune system and our psychological health as well. Lack of sleep seems to leave our perceptions more pessimistic. Studies confirm that people who get less sleep tend to remember negative stimuli more than the positive or neutral ones. Sleep also appears to play a critical role in processing trauma and preventing PTSD. Gulf War army truck drivers who were required to sleep had fewer symptoms than other combat groups. The bottom line is that about 8.5 hours is what we need to function and heal. People with taxing jobs and athletes often need even more sleep. Roger Federer, LeBron James, Usain Bolt, and Venus Williams all say they sleep ten to twelve hours a night. Many NBA players nap daily.

Lack of sleep also messes with our metabolism. If we don't get adequate sleep, we tend to crave more carbohydrates and sugar—perhaps for short-term energy—and satiety signals are disrupted, which leaves us hungry—particularly women and particularly in the evening, according to studies.

Cortisol, a stress hormone, also spikes when we're overtired. People who work nights appear to be more vulnerable to different forms of cancer, depression, heart disease, diabetes, and obesity. Lack of sleep may interfere with executive function and focus. Our body also learns how to sleep from the rhythms of the sun, making it important to get outside daily or at least to spend time near a window, which we know boosts mood. The effects of sleep deprivation on the brain are obvious to anyone who hasn't slept, but research finds that a bad night of sleep is almost like losing a few IQ points the next day, plus it makes focusing and managing emotions difficult.

Jacob, a client of mine who is an ice climber, broke dozens of bones in a bad fall—not on a frozen mountaintop in the Andes, but on the icy parking lot of a hotel in New Hampshire. After the accident, he was unable to sleep. (I should add that Jacob is extremely safety conscious when he climbs or teaches others.) A traumatic childhood had already set him up for self-blame, and after battling alcoholism as a young man, his love of climbing had become a healthy way to self-regulate and feel a sense of competence and embodiment—while still tapping into his nervous system's craving for healthy risk.

The psycological damage and pain was extensive, and because the fall was unrelated to climbing, the shame was pervasive. Jacob relived the moment again and again as his brain desperately sought to write a different ending to the story that didn't result in a humiliation. This is what our brains do: try to make a new, happy ending in which the trauma didn't happen. Even as his physical pain healed, he still couldn't sleep.

Jacob was a longtime meditator, but scanning and checking in with his body created *more* shame and anxiety at first, so he adapted his strategy. His body scans started with gratitude for where he didn't hurt, and tuned in to where he did. From there he began to practice relaxing his body, but at his own pace; relaxing too much did not feel safe. Next, he began to reconnect with ways his body could relax and he could re-inhabit his body more comfortably. Eventually his injuries healed and he began sleeping again. He nursed himself back to health with minimal help from opiates, which had nearly destroyed him as a young man.

Although a traditional, mindful body scan can be triggering for some people at first, a more active, progressive muscle relaxation practice can be grounding and soothing. When we are in the driver's seat of how relaxed we can be, the idea of relaxation is less scary. Here's a relaxation practice I learned form a colleague many years ago. For sleep especially, bodily comfort and relaxation are cues to our nervous system that we are safe.

The CALM Reminder

The CALM Reminder is adaptable to your time frame, attention span, and, most importantly, your own window of tolerance. It is as simple as its acronym, which stands for Chest, Arms, Legs, Mouth. When we can tune in to and relax the body, it offers up information about our emotional state so that we can respond rather than react. We feel more comfortable and at home in our body, welcoming and thanking our sensations. What's more, when you relax your body zone by zone, it becomes almost physiologically impossible to be stressed, anxious, angry, or otherwise flooded with difficult emotions. Through practice, we can begin to attend to and even befriend our bodies.

Adjust your body to a comfortable position, allowing your eyes to close if that feels comfortable. Begin with a few expanded breaths, allowing your body to relax as you extend the out-breath.

Chest

After a few breaths, bring your awareness into your **chest** and torso area. First scan your chest, opening it to create enough room for your lungs and belly to fully expand. Bring your awareness to any sensations in the chest, maintaining a curiosity for what they might be communicating.

Is your breath shallow and short, or slow and even? Is your heart beating fast or slow? Is there any tightness or tension in your chest? Feelings of warmth or coolness? What could any of these signals mean?

Finally, take a breath in and tense all the muscles throughout your chest and torso. Hold for a count of three as you notice what tension feels like, then allow your muscles to relax. Allow the tension to flow away and relaxation to flow in during the next few breaths as you extend gratitude to all the organs throughout your chest for keeping you alive.

Arms

Now direct your awareness into your **arms**, from your shoulders down to the tips of your fingers. Raise and drop your shoulders once, then allow your arms to fall to your sides or into your lap. Now scan your awareness upward from your hands and through your forearms and upper arms to your shoulders. Are your hands shaking or still? Can you allow them to settle if they are shaking? Are they tensed partly into fists? If so, just release that tension. Are your hands sweaty or clammy? Hot or cold? Scan up your arms to your shoulders, which often hold a lot of tension and emotion. Then continue to notice any other sensations that might offer clues to the state of your emotions or nervous system.

Finally, squeeze your fists, tense your arms all the way up to your shoulders, and hold for three breaths, feeling the tension. Then release both the physical and emotional tension, and let your arms relax completely. Take three more breaths, enjoying the newfound relaxation flowing into your arms, as you offer them gratitude for all they do for you.

Legs

On the next breath, direct your attention down to your **legs**—from your hips down through your toes—with awareness and breath flowing through your thighs, calves, and feet. Sometimes our legs can be bouncing with stress or holding tension tightly. Notice if your legs are communicating anything in this moment, and just allow them to become still if they are.

Next, gently begin to squeeze your muscles, starting in your feet and moving up through your legs and around your waist, holding that tension for three breaths. Note the sensations and release. Take three more breaths as you feel the tension flowing out of your legs, and offer thanks to your legs for the work they do.

Mouth

Shift your awareness to your **mouth** and jaw, where many of us hold emotional tension and clench our muscles without realizing it.

What expression is your mouth communicating inwardly and outwardly. Stress? Anxiety? Anger? Notice this and any other sensations in your mouth and jaw. You might expand that awareness to include the rest of your head and neck. Last, clench your mouth, jaw, and the muscles around it. Hold for three breaths before releasing.

As you let go of tension, you might allow your mouth to relax into a small smile if it feels natural. Thich Nhat Hanh reminds us that "sometimes your joy is the source of your smile, but sometimes your smile can be the source of your joy." And guess what? Research suggests the same. Take some time to enjoy the sensations of relaxation and smiling, and if you are feeling safer, you might allow yourself to sleep.

You dont have to do the CALM reminder before sleep, in fact, you might take time to reflect on where in your body you tend to hold which emotions, and you might adjust your body or breathe into those areas before finishing your practice. Remember, at any point in the day you can check in with your body and respond to what it needs.

To begin feeling comfortable in our lives, we can start by learning to befriend our bodies, breathing expansively, and filling our body to its edges. In movement or stillness—even in our imaginations—we can shift our moods by changing how we hold and carry our bodies. We can practice proactive self-care and self-compassion as we routinize eating and exercise to create the conditions for the deep, healing rest that the brain and body need to recover from trauma.

CHAPTER THREE

Your Resilient Mind

One of my first apartments had one of those smoke alarms that went off every time we burned the toast or steam billowed out of the bathroom after a hot shower. Suddenly, my roommates and I would jump out of our seats and scramble to silence the alarm, usually by tearing out the batteries. People with PTSD and anxiety can feel they have a smoke alarm like this in their minds. In a sense, they do. An overactive amygdala is like living with a smoke alarm in your brain that goes off every time you make toast. How well can you function when there's an alarm going off? Probably not very well!

When the amygdala is activated, cortisol and adrenaline spike—and so does testosterone. Together these lead to aggression and a lack of empathy. If you want to survive, you do *not* want to think about how cute and furry that lion chasing you is. You do *not* want to slow down to wonder if it just wants to cuddle! The primitive limbic system—your brain's alarm system—becomes activated, pulling blood into the amygdala and out of our more evolved outer cortices, including the prefrontal cortex, where we regulate emotion, control impulses, utilize critical thinking, and make long-term plans. If the alarm rings long enough, the brain recalibrates itself for the long term. Under chronic stress and long after, people may struggle with everyday tasks like making decisions, organization, and planning—in addition to other symptoms that can look like ADHD (attention-deficit/hyperactivity disorder).

When our best, most evolved brains are underpowered, we can't think straight or for very long, and we struggle to "make good choices," as I say to my six-year-old. The thoughtful, decision-making part of the brain goes offline, only to make impulsive, immediate decisions for short-term survival. We may even hear sounds at different frequencies, such as ringing in our ears. Our eyes dilate and perceive different colors and shapes. We may become more sensitive to smells and tastes than usual, often interpreting them as a danger. We look at neutral stimuli—people or ink blots on a page—and see trauma and threat everywhere, an experience known as hypervigilance. Even in safety—sometimes *especially* in safety—intrusive thoughts may arise, and we feel the urge to fight with rage, to panic and run, to collapse, or to numb out and hide where we won't be noticed.

This is the darker side of our brain's survival system, when we respond to stress with the four Fs. But remember that beyond the fight/flight/anxiety and freeze/faint/depression responses, the Attend and Befriend responses shift our brains as well. The science shows that as we practice mindful self-compassion, the amygdala gets smaller and less active. This is not like tearing the batteries out of the alarm; it's more like recalibrating it so that it goes off when a real danger is present, not a perceived one. We can retrain the brain back into the window of tolerance while simultaneously expanding it. Through mindfulness, compassion, and positive psychology, we can come into an optimal mental state for thriving rather than just surviving.

> **Mindfulness** has become a buzzword, but what is it, really? I define it as simply paying attention to our experience of the present moment with acceptance and nonjudgment, and trying to do that deliberately. **Mindful self-compassion** is the practice of recognizing and naming our experience of suffering. By connecting our suffering to the rest of humanity, we also recognize it as suffering and extend kindness to ourselves. Christopher Germer says we practice self-compassion not to feel better, but simply because we feel bad. **Positive psychology**, on the other hand, is the study and practice of flourishing and thriving beyond baseline survival.

As you practice the exercises in this chapter, you will activate and grow connections in important brain regions, even physically shrinking the brain's alarm system as it quiets down. The alarm will still go off, but only when there's an actual fire, not just smoke. You'll improve your ability to direct your attention, make choices, think critically, plan for the future, regulate your emotions, and truly respond rather than react to the world as it is. You will be able to self-monitor, get perspective, have empathy, understand what other people think, and not assume the worst. You'll improve your brain's ability to consolidate information from memory, which appears to be key in working through trauma. First, though, I bet you'd like some ways to turn off that fire alarm—or at least turn it down.

Fire-Alarm Reset Protocols

If you find your nervous system ramping up, you might try one of these simple, perceptual awareness exercises:

- Count the corners in the room.
- Notice everything around you that's the color green (or any other color).
- Note the shapes around you and the spaces between them.

- Even in a place where you have spent a lot of time, look around and see if you can notice something new, something that has changed, or something you've never noticed before.

- Take a tip from polyvagal expert Deb Dana and build anchors of safety into your space: colors, objects, and artwork that cue your nervous system to feel safe.

Using Your Words Is Mindfulness

Mindfulness practices soothe us at the physiological level, but it's not just about relaxing. In mindfulness meditation we name our emotions to activate the outer, more evolved, parts of the brain. There is a reason we tell kids to "use your words" when they are upset. Naming our physical and emotional experience as it arises activates the prefrontal cortex and quiets the limbic system back down, something that neuroscientists have watched happen in real time in brain imaging experiments. Psychiatrist Dan Siegel calls this phenomenon "Name It to Tame It."

When a therapist says something stereotypical like, "Sounds like you're feeling sad," they are helping you name and validate your emotions until you can do it for yourself. But naming and validating is something we can learn to do for ourselves. One of the best introductions and explanations of mindfulness comes from my colleague Brian Callahan, a fellow mindfulness teacher from Vancouver. Here's my adaptation of his approach to attending to our thoughts and emotions.

The Four Rs of Mindfulness

This practice shows us how mindfulness impacts our brains and teaches us how we can bring mindfulness to everything in our lives. The Four Rs are something we can practice both regularly, like a workout for your brain, or informally in any moment.

1. Rest — Begin by finding a place to rest your awareness. I prefer the word *rest*, as this practice should not feel like a huge effort. Think of an anchor, which effortlessly holds a boat in place while allowing it to drift, but not too far. Perhaps your anchor could be your breath or body, but if those are difficult, try an external anchor of awareness, such as focusing on sounds, scents, an image in front of you, a mental image, or the edges of your body rather than deep within your body.

2. Recognize — Soon enough, your mind will wander off, no matter how interesting or boring your anchor might be. In that moment, simply recognize the fact that your mind is wandering and give a name to the thought, such as "Thinking about my finances," "Feeling sad about Mom," or "That work issue again." In fact, *this* is the moment of mindfulness, not the fact that your mind has wandered but when you realize it. When you recognize where the mind has wandered, that's a moment of insight, getting to know your mind's habits. So the reality is not that mindfulness is keeping your mind perfectly still or thought-free. In fact, every time your mind wanders—even if it wanders a thousand times—it's just a thousand opportunities to practice mindfulness or a thousand insights into your own experience to respond more skillfully. The more you practice, the more you'll see what your mind (and body) do in different situations.

Each time you name where the mind has gone, you literally Name It to Tame It by quieting the limbic response, by directing blood to the outer cortices and out of the amygdala and the alarm system, and by strengthening the brain regions associated with self-regulation.

3. Return — Once you've noticed where and when your mind has wandered, gently guide your awareness back to your anchor. As you do this, you are "working out" your mental muscles by building capacity and connection in the prefrontal cortex where you regulate your attention.

Each time we direct our wandering awareness back with kindness and compassion, like a child or puppy who has wandered off, we practice building the muscle of self-compassion. If we can forgive ourselves for a little mind wandering in a moment of meditation when the stakes are low, we begin to forgive ourselves and be kind to ourselves in more challenging circumstances as well. The muscle of self-compassion continues to grow.

4. Repeat — Guess what? Your mind is going to keep wandering, so we just start fresh again with another cycle of the Four Rs of Mindfulness—constantly reborn in the present moment with another opportunity to practice.

Take five minutes, or thirty, or however many minutes you need to rest your awareness on some kind of anchor: breathing, sounds, sensations, or whatever you chose, and then recognize when your mind wanders and returns. Practice in small, safe amounts, ideally with someone you feel safe with. Stop if it gets too uncomfortable, and work up from there. You can rest, recognize, and return to your daily life—to walking, to eating, to working, to conversations—and in that way bring awareness and compassion to anything you do.

A few years back, I was leading a series of workshops in Argentina, and my host invited an American friend of a friend to attend one of the workshops—the kind of thing that happens in the small, expat world. Cameron came to dinner with a few other American expats and swapped some stories over an *asado*, Argentine barbecue. We were discussing some of the self-compassion practices, and Cam suddenly burst out with his story of how he'd ended up in Argentina. His breath became short and his body started shaking, almost convulsing. "I've never told you guys this," he blurted. "I'm here because my dad killed my mom and then killed himself. I left Michigan. I changed my name. I tried to get as far away as possible."

Like many expats I've encountered, Cameron was fleeing something, and despite his family's wealth and privileged background, the case made headlines beyond his small Midwestern community. Though Cam left behind his home, country, remaining family, and even his name, the trauma followed him. We had coffee the next day and have stayed intermittently connected since. He found the Four Rs helpful for bringing more presence to his life informally. "My mind would always wander back to that day I heard the news," he said. "And honestly it probably always will. But as I practiced the Four Rs, I could set those thoughts aside. They come back, for sure, but more and more I know when and where they tend to come, and they're less likely to overwhelm me the way they used to."

The Body Tames the Mind

It might seem strange to return to the body in a chapter about the brain. But the reality is that our brain, nervous system, and nerve endings are distributed throughout the entire body. This means, among other things, that our bodies are early warning systems. This is *neuroception*, the idea from polyvagal theory that we become aware of our emotions at the unconscious body level. Consider phrases like *It made my skin crawl, I got cold feet, I had butterflies in my stomach, My heart leapt,* and more. Or even more specifically, *I know in my heart* or *I had a gut feeling.* The more we learn about the vagus nerve, the more we see it extended into the very parts of the body that we associate with emotions and that send this very information back to the brain as an early warning.

One of the most profound experiences of my life was during my mid-twenties, when a friend snuck me into the cadaver lab at a local medical school. My initial fear and disgust slowly that gave way to a fascination as I saw that these human bodies were at once the most complex systems I'd ever seen, and simultaneously just simple piles of meat. My entire perspective on the shortness and fragility of life shifted. I experienced a sense of awe as well as an urgency to help others and to make a meaningful impact..

Shortly afterward, the Body Worlds exhibits came through town. I vividly remember one of the exhibits featuring just the blood-red outline of our nervous system stretched through the entire body. Until I saw that, I had never fully grasped the mind-body connection, which had always sounded so hokey. In glowing red, I was gazing at a map of the brain—not just in our skull but extending throughout the entirety of the human body, with particular density around the lungs, heart, and gut. My world, as the kids say, was shook.

The brain lives in the body and permeates it fully, from our sensory perception through our physical and even emotional responses and actions. And our bodies have protective mechanisms far beyond and far deeper than the physical.

A few years back, a young man from East Africa named Thomas came to see me while studying at Harvard's John F. Kennedy School of Government, often considered a finishing school for future world leaders. Thomas had spent years doing international relief work all over the world, and now he was getting a master's degree in public policy. An experience in his time abroad had left him scarred emotionally. While he was watching a soccer game at a popular café, a bomb tore through the restaurant. Thomas fled through the smoke to safety, crawling over body parts and patrons screaming in pain for help as they bled.

From that moment on, a few things in particular haunted Thomas. One was pervasive survivor's guilt; another was a hypervigilant, hair-trigger startle response. The slightest creak of the house at night, a door slamming at a party, or any sudden noise sent him right back to the fight-or-flight response from years before. It would take him a few minutes—or even hours—to reset his nervous system. It was starting to frighten his girlfriend.

Thomas didn't have an interest in or tolerance for an extended meditation practice, but we talked about the hypervigilance that would take him over, along with ways to self-regulate. In my office, we'd practice counting to five sounds, as if we were being deliberately hypervigilant. Thomas practiced at home and when walking into challenging or new situations, and he found it grounding. He said, "Doctor, it's like I'm in charge of my hypervigilance now. I can turn it on with this listening thing, and then I can turn it off," he explained. "It's not just turning on and taking over at random times to scare me and everyone around me."

It's easier said than done to "turn off" hypervigilance, but like these other aspects of our nervous system, if we can practice activating them, we can also practice deactivating them using the natural tools our bodies provide.

Sound Grounding

Here are a few ways to practice grounding with sound:

- **Sound Counting:** Rather than taking ten deep breaths, try counting up to ten sounds when you wake up, or at other transitional moments in your day.

- **Sound Zoom:** Take a few minutes and start listening to sounds far away, noticing one or two distant sounds. Then pay attention to closer sounds inside the building if you're indoors. Now listen closer still to sounds nearby, like your creaking chair. Then notice sounds of your own body—rustling clothes, your breath, the internal sounds of your heart or belly. You might even experiment with whether your thoughts have a sound.

- **Sounds Around:** Count a few sounds from each direction: left and then right, above and below, in front and behind, as well as any spaces and silences between sounds.

Of course, we have four other senses as well, and each is like a stone dropped in the pool of our thoughts and emotions, creating ripples. They are always in the present moment when we tune in to them. They anchor us and keep us from being pulled into the past or future.

Finding Safety in the Present Moment

It took me years of practicing mindfulness to truly appreciate the power and promise of the present moment, despite the thousands of books and memes extolling its virtues. For much of my life, my mind would spiral out of the present and into anxiety or depression. A typical thought stream might look something like: "I'm going to mess up this client, then they won't ever come back to my practice, and they'll tell everyone what a bad therapist I am, and then I'll go bankrupt, my wife will leave me, I'll probably die alone under a bridge, and no one will come to my funeral."

But when I practiced staying in the moment, I realized that I could still prepare for the future, like taking time to make a plan for working with someone, without getting caught up in a story of how badly it could go. The future is where anxiety usually resides. Think about it: most horror stories we tell ourselves are about events that haven't even happened—and probably never will. Or we find ourselves swept back to the past rather than into the future, reliving awful moments and relitigating with ourselves the shame we still feel. As Mark Twain never said, "I've experienced many terrible things in my life . . . only a few of which actually ever happened." There's another great fake quote, and this one *not* from Lao Tzu despite the frequent attributions: "Depression is living in the past; anxiety is living in the future. Peace can only be found in the present." I don't know who really said these things, but there's some truth to them.

> Our thoughts are often racing off to the past and future—about 48 percent of the time. That's so often that, statistically speaking, I should repeat it because half the readers probably glazed right over it. Yes, fully half the time, our minds are wandering to the past or the future—or they're comparing us to others, which we know doesn't usually go well. But when we check in with our senses, we can come right back to grounding ourselves in the present moment, where we are also happier. The same study that discovered our minds were wandering half the time also found that the more present we are, the happier we also are.

We can begin to explore the ways our perceptions impact our mood, our thoughts, and even the choices we make in the world. We can teach ourselves to check in with the present moment by getting in touch with our senses and emotions, with the thoughts and actions we want to take, and by learning how to manage that anxiety more effectively. I call it Taking a Mindful SEAT.

Taking a Mindful SEAT

Start in a comfortable pose, take a few extended breaths, and allow your eyelids to lower or even close if that feels comfortable. Then check in.

"S" Is for Senses and Sensations

Begin by checking in with your senses, starting with sounds. What sounds do you hear, near and far? Faraway sounds, closer sounds, the sound of your breath, even sounds from inside your body, like your heartbeat.

As you breathe, you might notice smells in the air: food, fresh air, and smells that are pleasant or unpleasant. On your tongue you might discover lingering tastes—or perhaps just a taste of the air.

Whether your eyes are open or closed, just notice what is in your field of vision as shapes, shadows, and colors, as well as the spaces in between these.

Last, bring your attention to sensations, starting at the edges of your body. Notice your back and legs resting on the seat behind and beneath you, the temperature of the air against your skin, and the texture of your clothing. If you feel comfortable, you might begin to explore sensations deeper in your body, just tuning in to sensations that ground you in the present, bringing you into the ventral vagal window of tolerance.

"E" Is for Emotions

Now shift your awareness toward your emotions as they arise and pass, perhaps even originating in sensations. What emotions are present in this very moment? Joy or sorrow? Anxiety or relief? Rage or peace? Boredom or curiosity or anything else? Just notice these emotions like they're visitors from beyond. Name them and watch as they arise and pass in both your body and your mind.

"A" Is for Actions

With an awareness of your senses and emotions, are there any urges or impulses to action that you notice? Do you want to stretch your body? Eat? Punch something? Make something or break something? Just notice these urges in your body and mind. These, too, you can watch pass.

"T" Is for Thoughts

Last, what thoughts are present right now? Any judgments about yourself or the world? Plans you are making? If you do notice your mind wandering, you can just nudge it back to the present.

Try the Mindful SEAT at different points in your day, both the easier and more difficult ones, and get to know your own mind, body, and triggers that much better. You might even write these out about a past event to get some perspective. Once we've identified these sensations as sensations, emotions as emotions, and thoughts and actions as just themselves, we empower ourselves with some perspective to make a healthy choice. It might look like this:

- Sense/Sensation: I can see an email in my in-box from my supervisor, I feel my heart pounding.

- Emotion: I'm scared he's going to reprimand me or even fire me!

- Action: I want to hide, close the email, and run out of the room.

- Thought: There must be something wrong with me . . . Or is there?

Once we've identified these sensations as sensations, emotions as emotions, thoughts and actions as just those, we can empower ourselves to get some perspective and make a different choice: perhaps a healthy-body choice like exercise, a self-compassion practice, a relational choice like reaching out to a friend, or another skill to relax and regulate your mind and body back to safety and thriving. As we slow down, we can watch our emotional responses arise first in the body, almost in real time. We can then offer ourselves compassion and choose a new response to what we encounter.

Don't Believe Everything You Think

There's that bumper sticker that says "Don't Believe Everything You Think," and while I'm a big fan of that in theory, it's far easier said than done. Still, one mental hack from Acceptance and Commitment Therapy expert Steven Hayes suggests making a top-ten playlist of some of your critical voice's greatest hits. Then, at the top of that list, add something like "I'm having the thought that . . ." Like most things in this book, I encourage you to start with small critiques so you won't overwhelm yourself.

I'm having the thought that . . .
I'll never get past this injury.
I'm having the thought that . . .
I'll never get to be healthy or happy.
I'm having the thought that . . .
I'll never have a romantic relationship again.
I'm having the thought that . . .
I'll be a bad parent and screw up my kids.
I'm having the thought that . . .
I'll never sleep through the night.

This exercise helps us see that we are not our thoughts. We learn that our critical voice isn't necessarily right, and then we can begin to cultivate a more compassionate inner voice that, in turn, helps us feel deserving of compassionate connection with others.

Gratitude Works

Gratitude gets a bad rap these days. The search for a silver lining is an easy one to toss onto the "toxic positivity" pile. It's true that forcing happiness when it's not there—or shoehorning happy endings onto a tragedy—helps no one and often leads to attacking ourselves with shame. But as humans, I believe we are capable of simultaneously holding both the ten thousand sorrows and the ten thousand joys of life, as Buddhism calls them. In fact, I believe we must.

I opened this book by explaining that post-traumatic stress and post-traumatic growth are not mutually exclusive. They can and do happen simultaneously. So too can difficulty and appreciation. Don't think this section is about what gratitude you can pull from your trauma or traumas. Instead, it's about what gratitude you can pull from your day or your week. Little by little, over and over, discovering what you're grateful for disrupts your brain's habit of seeing danger everywhere. When we practice gratitude, incredible changes happen in the brain and beyond. Gratitude can help lower anxiety and depression, improve physical health and life satisfaction, minimize aggression, maximize kindness, and help you sleep better and longer. All of these contribute to your recovery and growth.

Stress, trauma, anxiety, and depression make our natural negativity bias even worse. Everyone and everything looks like a threat: my boss is about to fire me, my wife is about to leave me, that person on the dating app looks like a mess. These are shortcuts that we think create more safety. This leads to more anxiety and depression, or it revs up past issues like trauma or addictions in new ways. But in the modern world, just knowing that you have a negativity bias is empowering and helps you to "not believe everything you think," as the bumper sticker suggests. Gratitude helps us rebalance.

One client who had lost her house and most of her possessions in a wildfire told me, "Gratitude is not putting on rose-colored glasses. It's more like taking off the shit-covered glasses." In that way, as my friend Chris Germer describes it, gratitude is a wisdom practice that helps us see more clearly. Gratitude can even boost creativity and help us see opportunities for growth that we might otherwise overlook. Gratitude is not about pretending the hard stuff isn't there. In a sense, it's about learning to appreciate sunshine and trees on our walk while also watching out for the dog shit we're about to step in.

So how can we practice gratitude? Let me count the ways. The first is an extended visualization, inspired by my friend Rick Hanson's practice, Take In the Good.

Taking In the Good

Spend a moment to settle in by lengthening your exhale or getting in touch with the moment in whatever way works best for you.

Now look back over your day so far. What was a good moment? A small success? A moment of pleasure? This can be small: a good cup of coffee, your comfy couch, a fun text from a friend. Who was there at that moment, and what was the scene? Take some time to bring the images to mind, maybe even recalling sounds, smells, and your other senses. Cultivate not just the facts but the feelings and the experience of the good memory.

Sit with this image in your mind—and your physiological experience of it. Tune in to your body and savor the sensations as they arise, not just in your mind. As you savor this image, dopamine (a "reward" neurotransmitter) and oxytocin are released. A slight smile might naturally form on your mouth, but there's no need to force it.

Continue to rest your awareness on the sensations as you raise your eyes and tune back in to your surroundings.

As you finish, you might take a moment to reflect about this experience: write, doodle, or otherwise express what came up.

So what happened in that practice? We disrupted, in mind and body, the negativity bias's automatic, autonomic takeover with an active practice, steering us out of passive negativity. Just as we have a physiological response when we recall stress, we can have one when recalling a positive experience as well—but it takes practice to cultivate and encode. Although the research indicates that within seconds, one negative experience is encoded into how we perceive the world, a positive experience takes a minute or two to encode. That's why we did the drawn-out visualization with writing afterward. Even more helpful for keeping the feeling alive is to share our gratitude. Reach out and text a friend about your good moment, or thank them if they were a part of it. Happiness or gratitude is amplified by sharing.

It's far too easy for us to connect around something negative. A gratitude group or chain helps us to connect around the positive. I'm in a social media group with some friends who share a few things a few times a week, inspiring each other, or maybe nudging each other, to post as a way of reminding us all that—wow!—the trees are beautiful today. My best friend from middle school, Gabe, gave a talk about how he and a friend had sent each other fifteen thousand texts of gratitude over the years. You can make gratitude a daily or annual ritual by bringing it into family gatherings besides Thanksgiving. We can also thank other people we feel grateful for— more about that in the next chapter.

Our culture right now is so binary, telling us it's one way or the other, all good or all terrible. A traumatized brain falls into that pattern, too. Meditation teacher and coach Jessica Morey reminds us to practice AWE, an acronym that stands for And What Else. Painful emotions might be happening here and now, but we can always ask ourselves, *And What Else* is here? During or after trauma, we tend to tune in to danger everywhere, amplifying the negativity bias and survival energy. You might always track the exits or know where your keys and phone are at every moment or where the nearest police station is—either to find it or avoid it. With gratitude, you can still do that, but you can also tune in to the good and accurately find the safety signals. What starts as an active process becomes an unconscious habit that helps us heal.

If you are stuck, try categories of gratitude: people, places, and things you are grateful for. Or, challenge yourself by reflecting on your own strengths and likable qualities. If it's a person you are grateful for, boost your mood by reaching out and thanking them. Go ahead and try it now: thank someone who gave you the time or money to read this book, then notice how it feels before, during, and after you expressed your gratitude.

When I know I have to make a gratitude list at the end of the day, I just start noticing those beautiful things around me. This is when the brain goes into what's called "cognitive priming," collecting positive things in spite of itself, like Velcro. This lifts our mood and shifts our perspective a bit more toward the positive. It's like finding a twenty-dollar bill in a winter jacket the next fall. It was there all spring and summer—you always had it—but when you find it, you're still psyched.

Rather than either/or, gratitude can help water the seeds of both/and in our journey toward growth. Over time, you might find yourself seeking out more positive things, consciously or unconsciously bringing joy to your day as you deliberately read happier, healthier news stories, take the scenic route home, and treat yourself occasionally. My friend and fellow therapist Linda Graham suggests that just as we take medication to "stay ahead of the pain," so too can we practice gratitude to stay ahead of the misery.

I want to return to the story of Thomas and a final, particularly challenging category of gratitude and appreciation. Long after Thomas's nervous system had settled after surviving the bombing, he remained plagued by guilt. Why had he just run away? He also asked me, and perhaps himself: Why hadn't he stopped to help the strangers or even friends who had been at the café? Years later he was still trying to outrun the survivor's guilt and, for that matter, the guilt for his own flight response. He berated himself, holding his head in his hands: "What kind of person just leaves everyone else bleeding and runs away?"

The first injury for Thomas to work through was the trauma itself. The second was his self-blame, shame, and survivor's guilt. Thomas was experiencing something like what psychologists call "moral injury," which is when we do something—or are forced or coerced to do something—against our values. Moral injury is a common experience in war veterans and other survivors of trauma or domestic violence.

I tried to explain that the fight/flight reaction is not usually one we can control in the crisis; it's hardwired into us. The Attend/Befriend responses are built into us as well, but they might take time to cultivate. Thomas was unfailingly polite, if skeptical, and I could tell he only sort of believed me. When he despaired that he must be a psychopath because he had left others behind, I wondered aloud, "Would a psychopath feel guilty for years about something?" Small cracks began to appear in Thomas's guilt and self-blame, aided by some self-compassion practices and by cultivating gratitude and appreciation toward his own strengths.

I asked him to list what he liked about himself and what he viewed as his strengths. It was far from easy for him. It helped when he took the perspective of what others appreciated about him. By looking from the outside, he was able to begin to appreciate some of his strengths. He also tapped into his religious beliefs, to what strengths God might have given him.

"I am a good friend—extremely loyal," Thomas offered.

"Go on," I encouraged him.

"I'm smart, or at least people think I'm smart enough to be here for school."

"Either way," I responded, "that's a gift to put to use, although as your therapist I do happen to think you are smart."

"Okay…" he said. "I have to admit, this feels very strange, doctor."

It might feel strange, unfamiliar, or even narcissistic to explore our strengths, depending on our background and cultural messaging. It's especially hard when we are used to feeling bad about ourselves; it can feel uncomfortable to name the good. If you can tolerate it, welcome that discomfort, acknowledge those doubts, and ask them to step back. Because why should it be more strange to dwell on our strengths than our flaws? The catch-22 was that survivor's guilt made Thomas feel bad whenever he felt good, yet he was comfortable with—or at least familiar with—the survivor's guilt. Gradually, though, this could begin to shift.

I encouraged Thomas—and I encourage you—to make a list of your strengths. Reflect on the awkwardness and joy that arises, and perhaps ask a loved one to help. It can be hard to do. Thomas ultimately made a good list for himself, which included being smart, hard-working, and loyal to friends and family. All of these strengths were powerful in the service of his last strength, which was also his career—his dedication to others, to going home to make his country better and stronger. Thomas saw the metaphor before I did: how his healing paralleled the healing he wanted to bring back to his homeland, which was fragmented by civil strife in the postcolonial wars that had roiled his country. What's more, the work was meaningful to him, and therefore healing. It was by finding meaning that growth beyond the trauma began for him.

Gratitude for Your Strengths

Take out a piece of paper and reflect on a few of your strengths—perhaps those that have helped you in hard times. If it helps, you may take an outside perspective by asking yourself, What do my friends or others appreciate about me? You may even find some inspiration by taking the University of Pennsylvania's positive-strengths inventory to learn a bit more about yourself. (See Citations by Chapter on page 154). Notice how the process feels, any resistance to doing it that arises, and any shift that may occur during and after.

Just like Thomas, your mind might also make up stories about what could have been different or what you should have done or said. Again, we tend to point that negativity bias at ourselves. And the worst part is the negativity bias will tell you stories about what you could have done differently, because it thinks you had control somehow. I want to emphasize that that's a natural and common response, but it's not particularly helpful. In fact, sometimes negativity will cheer on that self-blame with voices of the larger society as the chorus. It would be simple to say *Ignore that voice*, but I know and you know that's easier said than done. What might be more helpful is to learn to listen to other voices, inside and out, as we practice more self-compassion.

Tending to the Mind and Body

During and after a trauma, the brain constricts to anticipate danger with an even more active negativity bias. But when we start with mindfulness and other practices, we can activate the entire brain, processing the world and our emotions with more perspective and clarity. We can also stay present with what is and truly respond rather than react. Over time, as we choose new responses to our challenges, we rewire our brain for more resilience as we go forward.

We can slow down and watch our emotions arise in the body through practices like the Mindful SEAT, or we could bring ourselves back to the present through the Four Rs of Mindfulness in formal and informal ways. Gratitude and appreciation help us see the hope even in the midst of challenges, and we can begin to practice forgiving ourselves.

Now I want to offer one more way you can cultivate the skills to respond to your needs as they arise in real time and to balance yourself physically, mentally, and relationally.

In my early twenties, I was miserable. More miserable, I think, than most of us at that age. My own traumas—combined with doing underpaid, exhausting work with sex offenders in a chaotic environment—were taking their toll. I still lived a mostly collegiate lifestyle, just without the substances. Exercise? Forget it. Breakfast and lunch? Why bother? (Plus I was too cheap.) Sleep? I'd stay up late and sleep in. When a friend in a Twelve-Step Program suggested that caring for my basic needs might start changing my mood, I thought such a simple solution was far too obvious to work.

However, when I started treating food, exercise, and sleep like medicine, it began to make a huge difference in my mood and outlook. I'm not going to suggest that tweaking these things will fix everything, but it's an important place to start.

HALT

You know already that your brain, body, and interpersonal relationships are readily dysregulated. Try a quick, easy check-in called HALT to see how you are doing and what you need to truly attend to in order to befriend your brain and body. **HALT** is an acronym to bring more awareness to your basic needs: Hungry, Angry/Anxious, Lonely, Tired.

What I love about HALT is the solid science behind it. Without this basic physical and emotional self-care, our nervous system is likely to betray us. Let's examine each one at a time.

Hungry: The prefrontal cortex—where our impulse control, emotion regulation, critical thinking, and decision-making reside—is a serious gas-guzzler. A shortage of calories will lead to a shutdown in these important brain abilities. Check in with your body's hunger signals regularly, listening to what it needs physically in terms of sustenance, not just what it wants emotionally. Remember, not every meal has to be perfect; self-denial is not self-compassion. You can practice some self-indulgence and pleasure even while practicing self-compassion. Eating on a routine will also cue your body to sleep later in the day.

Angry/Anxious: If emotions like anger are "fight," and anxiety is "flight," then feeling angry *and* anxious means we are operating from our limbic system, the most primitive part of the brain and nervous system. Remember, these strong emotions shut down blood flow to the parts of the brain that think and reason, leading us to react rather than respond.

If emotions are running high, consider a few slow, mindful breaths to quell the limbic system and activate the outer cortices of the brain, where we can think clearly again. You can also simply "name to tame" the strong emotions, just noting them as they appear in your mind or body. Wherever you feel strong emotions—body or mind—simply name them as they arise and activate your best brain. Other sensory grounding practices like feeling your feet can also help here.

Lonely: There's another self-help slogan I love: "If your mind is a dangerous neighborhood, don't go there alone." As social animals, we humans are susceptible to tribalism, groupthink, toxic emotional contagions, and mob mentality, but loneliness has its dangers, too. Introverts and extroverts have differing optimal social set points, but we all need to strike a balance between solitude and socializing. Explore the best balance for you. Friendships and community are directly correlated with happiness, mental health, physical health, even longevity. What's more, a healthy support network validates and encourages us to follow through with our recovery. (There's more on healthy relationships in chapter 4.)

Tired: Yup, when we're tired, either from overworking or undersleeping, our self-control, mood, and judgment slip away. A poor night's sleep can knock your psychological and physical immune system down a peg, and it also reduces judgment and impulse control. Evidence shows that consistent sleep—at approximately the same bedtime and waking time—might be as or more important than the total amount. So consider some basic, healthy sleep habits as integral to your self-care. To settle your system before sleep, place your hand on your heart or practice the CALM Reminder. Also, be sure to give yourself a chance to rest in a restorative way during a busy day.

CHAPTER FOUR

Your Resilient Heart

We need people the most during and after a trauma, yet the invisibility of many traumas—especially those associated with illness, injury, or shame—cuts us off from others. For instance, as my mother got sicker, her world grew smaller, and so did mine. Was it okay to tell people about her illness? How much could I tell? When and how? When others shared this part of my life with their communities, I felt violated and more isolated; it wasn't always their story to tell, or they didn't tell *my* truth of it. I learned for myself what many have discovered: stress and trauma impact our interpersonal lives in particularly insidious and heartbreaking ways.

Trauma isolates, and too much isolation traumatizes further. Illness and injury physically separate us, and the emotional experience of them can make it hard to relate to others. Abusive relationships isolate us by design, both during the abuse and with the shame long after. We often speak differently in response to trauma by utilizing a smaller range of vocal tones and by making smaller movements and fewer facial expressions. Why? So as not be noticed and to avoid the risk of another traumatic attack. Or we might speak and act aggressively to fend off would-be attackers. I think often of the saying, "Not fragile like a flower, fragile like a bomb," which can be an embrace of gentle power or reflect the more explosive nature of some people's trauma response.

In a true crisis, we need to identify who or what is dangerous so we know whether to attack or escape. Under traumatic stress, we therefore can't take other people's perspective; we become more self-absorbed in order to be self-protective, which in turn makes us more anxious and depressed. Our ability to empathize or to offer a second chance shuts down in order to keep us safe. We even notice our physical discomfort more.

All of these perfectly understandable responses wreak havoc on our relationships with families, partners, friends, and colleagues when we fight or flee from them. Those responses can also skew our ability to trust. We end up more isolated—a huge physical and mental health risk factor. To stay safe relationally, we either shrink into isolation or overcompensate with aggression, fearing judgment or rejection of others. This jumpstarts that critical inner voice we all have, sending us deeper into a spiral of shame and isolating us even more when we need just the opposite.

Connecting is actually a baby's first form of stress regulation according to many researchers, including Stephen Porges, a proponent of polyvagal theory. You can observe this in children: first they try socially to engage their wants or dislikes, then they react with a fight-or-flight response, then they often freeze and give up, as demonstrated in the popular video "the still face experiment" on YouTube. Under threat, we first engage the ventral vagal, calm-centered social system, with breath and heart rate slow and regular, before trying fight-or-flight activation of the sympathetic nervous system. Then we go into a freeze-or-faint response with dorsal vagal activation as we give up and withdraw. The point is that our earliest and probably best medicine for self-regulation is other people. More specifically, well-regulated, healthy people, including partners, family members, friends, work colleagues, support groups, and—yes—therapists.

Trauma makes us feel alone, and sometimes it literally leaves us alone. Feelings of safety are inhibited when cortisol clogs our receptors for oxytocin, the neurohormone that allows us to feel safe, secure, and attached. Oxytocin also helps us read facial expressions and emotions, understand others, and build empathy and trust. Alternatively, loneliness and isolation elevate cortisol, another neurohormone, which is linked to poor health and shorter lifespans. High cortisol levels are as bad for our health as smoking or obesity; they also correlate with anxiety and depression and are linked to addiction.

Healthy co-regulation, on the other hand, becomes a shared sense of safety. I signal safety to you, you feel safe, and vice versa. But that takes work. Over time, we get into what my colleague Deb Dana describes as "safe rhythms of regulation" with other people. At first, you need others to help you do this, but with practice you can regulate yourself. Ultimately you can offer it to others. Examples of co-regulation are at a sporting event when everyone cheers together or during concerts or comedy shows, where audience members laugh or sing together. Everyone is getting doses of dopamine and serotonin in sync. We do this on a smaller scale when we sit around the dinner table with friends or family. We co-regulate one-on-one with our therapists and colleagues, or when we smile at the checkout clerk and mean it. We even co-regulate with our pets, whose presence can cue our calm because they can serve as an external fight-or-flight system for us. And, of course, we all hope to co-regulate with our children and with anyone else we care for.

Four Roses, a Thorn, and a Bud

During the pandemic, my family began to practice Roses and Thorns before bedtime, or sometimes around the dinner table. I learned this gratitude ritual at a job that was knee deep in trauma all week long. We practiced with both the staff and the kids in treatment every Friday.

The practice is simple. The negativity bias lands at about a four-to-one ratio, so each person takes a turn sharing four "roses" (good things) from their day, one "thorn" (a disappointment), and one "bud" (hope) for tomorrow.

One of the "roses" of the whole pandemic was that our family was together enough to make this a regular practice. My son, ever eager to delay bedtime, often advocates for a hundred roses!

Much of post-traumatic growth happens in community, where we can be co-regulated, witnessed, and supported by others. Like any ailment, trauma can heal on its own with time, but when healed with others, it's far less likely to leave scars or lasting psychic damage. The social engagement system creates a positive spiral. More trust leads to more connection, which is linked to happiness, thriving, and mental and physical health.

Recent research has made it ever more clear that emotions, moods, and behaviors are contagious. Some scientists call this "interpersonal neurobiology"; others have studied the ways "mirror neurons" create an emotional give-and-take through the thousands of microexpressions revealed in our faces each second. Still others explain this as the collective nervous system that regulates and dysregulates in sync with others, impacting our thoughts, feelings, and behaviors. With practice, we can jumpstart the social-engagement system for our own connection and healing, cultivating a "neuroception of safety."

Healing Is Other People

Our responses to trauma can make it hard to create a robust social support network.. Sometimes trauma has the effect of making dangerous people and behaviors feel trustworthy, while making friendly people and safe situations feel unfamiliar, and thus dangerous. The physical and emotional vulnerability that comes with intimacy sets off alarms, and friendly people may then seem threatening. As the nervous system settles into an avoidant autopilot, we may feel—perhaps accurately—that other people will never fully get what we've experienced, that we won't "feel felt."

I had a client many years ago whose mother died while driving drunk. Eight-month-old Amanda was found hours after the accident, still crying in the car seat, while her mother bled out in the driver's seat. The attachment trauma was there. The shock trauma. The relational trauma and the loss. But what adult Amanda also carried was the shame: her own and her mother's. "It's like I've got this giant thing I'm carrying with me that no one else can see, even though most people keep almost bumping into it. When do I tell a new girlfriend that my mom died? The first date? The fourth? And then when do I tell them *how* she died? It's too big to share, but it's too big *not* to share. Anytime the conversation gets close to this, my heart pounds and my body literally heats up, so I just stopped bothering to connect with people. I don't want to traumatize them either— no one knows what to say to me about my mom. And then after every breakup, I'm always left wondering if it was because I shared too much or if they could tell I was hiding."

After a series of bad relationships and escalating drug use of her own, Amanda finally began to connect with a community in Alcoholics Anonymous. Like many people in recovery from addiction, trauma was a part of her story and, like many, her own addiction created more trauma: accidents, overdoses, and violence. In her recovery group, she found women who identified with her experiences and a place where she could be heard and not judged on her path to healing.

Support networks are key to feel connected and part of a community. Small pods of thirty to forty trusted people balance us, including the regulars at your coffee shop, gym, or salon, and your adult kickball league. As for online communities, research says about 150 "friends" in our social networks is optimal, but people with more than 150 friends are more likely to feel unhappy and unsupported. Support groups, recovery meetings, spiritual communities, and even healthy workplaces can help us heal. We need a space to tell our truth, and although there's never a perfectly safe space, there are safer ones. It takes courage and hard work to find your people—but you can.

We all have different set points between introversion and extroversion, so see for yourself what level of social interaction serves you. I worked with an introvert who had isolated even more deeply after the traumatic loss of a friend. He said, "I don't always like going out with people, but I always feel better when I do. It's like medicine—I have to make myself do it sometimes because I know I'll feel better later. I know that isolating is an early-warning system just like stopping my medication." Like my client, you might find this to be true for you as well; I know it's true for me. As we enter compassionate communities, we allow others to love us until we can love ourselves.

After a trauma, it can be hard to learn how to trust others again, even those friends who try to support us. Psychotherapist and grief advocate Megan Devine writes this about grief: "This is exactly as bad as you think it is. And people, try as they might, really are responding to you as poorly as you think they are." Eventually, though, you will find your people, and you truly don't need many, just a few.

When we heal ourselves, we heal others—just through our presence. As my friend Dr. Sará King says, "Anytime we come together with two or more people, we form a collective nervous system. Our bodies are designed to share with one another the wealth of our homeostasis—our physiological, psychological, and relational well-being—from the time we are in the womb."

Resilience Is Resistance

I want to acknowledge that daily relational trauma may be a fact of life for you to due to racism, sexism, or other systemic injustices. Author bell hooks wrote, "Being oppressed means the absence of choices." A lifetime of doors slammed shut, of marginalization and rejection, adds up to trauma that affects us as much as a physical blow. And the trauma of anyone in our community reverberates out to all of us. An injury to one nervous system is an injury to our collective nervous system. Yet, when we speak our truth to others, we become less alone and can move toward action and justice.

"Silence = Death" was the cry during the 1980s for people traumatized by both AIDS and bigotry. In 2018, millions of women found sisterhood and support against harassment and sexual assault by joining the #MeToo movement. Protestors chanting in unison that "Black Lives Matter" synchronized their bodies and minds in a call for justice. Returning veterans are speaking more openly about traumatic brain injury and demanding recognition of combat stress and military sexual assault. In each of these movements, people built alliances of compassion and understanding in their immediate circles and within the larger culture as well. As a patient who attended an assault survivor's group told me, "I go to the group to get better; I stay in the group to help others." Safe affinity groups are key to healing and growth.

Activism is one way to channel what happened to you, although public protests and the like may not be for everyone. I've worked with many trauma survivors who turned their suffering into action, including women and men who stood up to the clergy who abused them, survivors who organized for gun safety after a mass shooting, and campaigners for better health care after they coped with illness.

Sadly, many reported that the bullying and death threats they faced when they stood up were worse than the original trauma, and some said they might not publically protest again. Some felt objectified as activists when they were put on a pedestal and expected to be superhuman or perfect. "People see me as either a hero or a villain," said a political activist whom I consulted with about mental health and self-care. "Neither of those is what I am, which is just a human being—a kid trying to change the world and finish grad school and deal with a long-distance relationship and annoying parents." Although starting a campaign or joining a movement might be right for some people, for you, *just your resilience is resistance*. If trauma is about a lack of choice or power, the more choices you have for your own path to healing, the more empowered you are in a moment or for a lifetime.

> Relational trauma is literally painful to us. Recent research from Japan suggests that isolation and rejection activate the same neural circuits as physical pain. Loneliness and isolation elevate cortisol and are linked to worse health outcomes and shorter lifespans, and they are as detrimental to health as smoking or obesity. Loneliness and isolation also correlate with anxiety and depression, and these emotional states are linked with addiction.

Self-Compassion and the Critical Voice

A few years back, a researcher surveyed a thousand random people from across the United States with the question, "Who is your worst enemy?" The resounding answer from half the surveyed participants was "Myself." Every honest person I've ever met—trauma survivors, therapists, Fortune 500 CEOs, Oscar winners—has described what they call their "inner critic," that voice we all have that tells us we aren't good enough, no matter how many accomplishments we have. Oh, and if it wasn't clear, I do, too.

If you've survived trauma or neglect, that critical voice is likely to be even louder or harder to ignore. It might echo abusive caregivers or bullies; it might echo abusive bosses or partners. It might echo the larger society by saying, *You don't belong,* or *There's something wrong with you because of the color of your skin, where you're from, or how you express your gender, culture, or any other identity markers.* These, as well as those voices that dismiss or belittle your trauma, deliberately or not, have become internalized as your critical voice, often at a young age. But when you start to practice self-compassion and work with your critical voice, you can more readily begin to make compassion connections outside of yourself as well, supporting your recovery and journey through life. You might try this self-compassion break, created by Christopher Germer and Kristin Neff, which I've adapted for you here.

The Self-Compassion ACE Up Your Sleeve

A Acknowledge the difficulty of the moment.

C Connect yourself to the larger human experience.

E Extend yourself whatever compassion you need in the moment.

Find yourself a comfortable, mindful posture that you can sustain for about ten minutes or so.

In the first part of this practice, recall a time when that critical voice was active. As always, start small: running late for a meeting, a foot-in-mouth moment, or a time you didn't speak up when you wish you had. Maybe you ate too much ice cream or not enough kale. We all have those little moments.

Bring the scene to mind: Who was there? What happened? How did you feel in your body and mind? What was your critical voice saying? With what words? With what kind of tone? Simply notice all of this, and then . . .

Acknowledge this experience. Find words and a tone that resonate for you and a more compassionate inner voice—the kind you would offer a friend, child, or someone you care about—to validate the experience. For instance:

That sounds hard.
This is a difficult moment.
This feels bad.

Take a few minutes to offer yourself a few

words of validation, perhaps things you would want someone who cares about you to say. The important thing is for the words and tone to feel genuine and that it's what you need to hear, not what you think you *should* say.

In the next part, begin to humanize the experience . . .

Connect your experience to others with some words that resonate:

No one is perfect.
We all make mistakes.
Pencils have erasers.
We all fall short some days.

Once again, find the words and tone that you would want to hear.

Finally;

Extend yourself some empathy and kindness with a more compassionate voice. Again, be sure to use the kind of words we might offer a friend or child. This might even include the gentle touch of a hand on your heart, a gentle hug, or a hand on your shoulder—just like you might offer a friend. Find again the supporting words:

May I forgive myself.
May I let this go.
May I be patient with myself.
May I learn from this.

Take a few minutes to allow all of these phrases to land and really sink in. When you are ready, open your eyes. Notice if there has been any shift in your mind and body.

As always, try this with small things and then see if you can apply it in a moment of need. One client, who was back home for the holidays and was triggered by his family's drinking, offered himself more colorful phrases like:

A: This is an absolute batshit moment of holiday insanity.

C: We all struggle with in-laws—to the point that it's become a cliché for comedians.

E: May I give myself a break and enjoy the food and keep my family safe.

As much as my client wanted to shrink and hide from the drunk in-laws, what really helped him through the weekend was taking an occasional break by escaping to the bathroom, where he re-inhabited his body by sitting up straight and offering himself affection and kindness.

Self-compassion practices like ACE may feel strange or self-conscious at first, especially if we haven't experienced a lot of feeling safe with ourselves or others. New feelings can set off alarm bells or create a "backdraft" and slam shut the window of tolerance. Go slowly, have some grounding practices at the ready, and—most importantly—be authentic with yourself.

According to the research, you need a therapist who feels authentic and present in order to get work done. One client told me she stuck with me because I "didn't give off a fake Mr. Rogers vibe." While I love Mr. Rogers, I guess it was a compliment of my authenticity. You also need your inner, compassionate voice to feel just as authentic so that you can be present for yourself and build that safe, secure attachment to yourself. Find the voice and tone that works for you; it may even be firm, but it needs to be compassionate. The key is finding words and a tone that resonate with you, like your own inner therapist. The words you use for yourself should be the same ones you'd offer a friend or, better yet, a child.

Affirmations

Do positive affirmations work? Most trauma survivors know a bullshitter when they see one, and trying to bullshit yourself with empty affirmations, the science says, makes us feel even worse. One study finds that if you have high self-esteem, affirmations rate somewhere between harmless and helpful, but if you already feel bad about yourself, affirmations will likely make you feel worse.

Research shows that self-compassion is correlated with healthier risk-taking, putting ourselves out there, and bouncing back from failure. We become more optimistic and even creative as we become confident enough to take action, to feel proud of our actions, and to let go of outcomes, at least a little bit. Self-compassion breaks are particularly helpful when we put a lot of pressure on ourselves to perform perfectly.

My client Rima lives in Abu Dhabi, in the United Arab Emirates. She grew up in Detroit, the child of displaced refugees from the Middle East. Her parents' trauma spilled over to her, and Rima grew up with numerous adverse childhood experiences and traumas. Now that she's the vice president of a health-care system in the region, she simply cannot feel that she "deserves" to be in her position; instead, she puts impossible expectations on herself. She reads every email from colleagues as criticism, and she writes off every compliment she receives as irrelevant. Such high self-monitoring is a common form of anxiety in trauma survivors and in women in the workplace. And the "spotlight effect"—thinking others notice us more than they do—is typical as well.

Rima and I together practiced reading and savoring the positive emails she received, and we discussed her role in effecting positive change at the company. This helped her nervous system shift to more empowerment as she owned her successes and put herself out there more.

We worked on self-compassion and on letting go of her need to be the perfect mother to four children, the perfect wife to her successful husband, and the perfect female administrator in a challenging culture that was only partially her own. Rima told me recently that after twenty years of meditation, it took just a few years of self-compassion for her inner critic to evolve in a positive way. "Meditation and yoga were super helpful to just calm me down in the world," Rima said. "But self-compassion was what really shifted the negative self-talk, which sounded a lot like my abusive dad, if I'm honest. I still get angry with myself, but now, on my absolute worst day, I say, *Ugh, you bozo*, to myself instead of *You fucking asshole! Why can't you do anything right?* Progress, not perfection I guess. And honestly, it's a lot like my worst day with the kids. It almost feels like I'm re-parenting myself."

A little self-compassion can go a long way toward helping us begin to quiet that critical voice we all have. Try the ACE self-compassion break. Try reading those complimentary emails with someone who knows you and can reinforce their message. Try doing something creative but challenging that you're good at and that makes an immediate impact. Once you become less critical of yourself, you can start to connect more readily with others without the self-consciousness of the critical voice chattering away and inhibiting your social connections.

Better Boundaries

Recently, I heard a friend say, "Self-care and self-compassion are not just bubble baths and bonbons; they're also setting good boundaries." I couldn't agree more. Boundaries empower us. Not as a power over others, but in a power *from* others. We become empowered with the choice to decide how much power other people, places, and things hold in our lives. In turn, we can choose how much they influence and impact our own thoughts, feelings, and behaviors. We begin to approach the world in a new way, with confidence and compassion, focusing on the potential, power, and relief it can bring.

Trauma almost always involves trampling—and sometimes smashing—physical, emotional, and relational boundaries around what we once thought was safe. When anything is broken, it takes time to build back. However, our nervous system often hastily rebuilds what was broken without our conscious input. This is done to keep us safe, but the result is often a patched-together protection with a "neuroception" alarm system that overperceives danger and seeks to appease or avoid conflict, which leaves us resentful, regretful, or both.

Because boundaries have been broken, after a trauma it is often hard to discern when our boundaries are being violated. We may feel we need to please or appease others, isolate ourselves for protection, or surprise and scare ourselves and others with an emotional explosion at the wrong moment when an interpersonal booby trap has been approached.

I think of boundaries in two ways: positive and negative. Negative boundaries—things we ask people and ourselves not to do—can be hard to set when we've been conditioned to not say no. Practicing by starting small and adjusting your posture and voice may help. Still, these boundaries are important to set *clearly* from the beginning of a relationship and then ease up as you feel safe. Setting boundaries both shows and tells the other person what you will and won't, can and can't, do. Dan Siegel recommends mindfully tuning in to your body as you practice saying either "no" or "yes." Notice the discomfort or comfort with each statement, as a means of practicing and building up a tolerance for learning how to assert yourself. In fact, with practice the amygdala will get less active with each "no," and saying "no" will start to feel safe, comfortable, empowering, and fun. Likewise, you can practice tuning in to your body as you move through the world and tuning in to people as they enter your personal space. Often we feel a tightening around our gut when our physical boundaries are pushed.

Positive boundaries are when we tell people what we are willing do and when, and they may be easier for those of us who struggle to say "no" clearly and confidently. This is a technique I recommend a lot in couples therapy. For instance, saying "I can talk to you about this tomorrow after the kids are asleep," is more effective and specific than stonewalling or blowing up. This also invites you and the other person to really show up for the conversation fully when it's time, and it shows you are a reliable, stable attachment and connection figure.

Reclaiming Time

Time can distort and slip away from us after a trauma. You might have noticed your brain struggling to process time effectively during and after traumatic events, such as how our days shifted into "blursday" during a pandemic lockdown. I suggest setting a time boundary for yourself, a routine to make life predictable, especially when you have free time. This actually saves limited resources for our prefrontal cortex. If your mind feels like a dangerous place to go alone, it's helpful to know who and what's coming to fill the anxiety or emptiness of an overscheduled or unplanned day.

Rigid routines may be helpful for some, and they perhaps explain why some inherently trauma-inducing jobs, like positions in the military, focus on structured time and timeliness. Not all of us, however, are built for or capable of following rigid structures. Instead of setting a strict schedule—wake at eight o'clock, shower at eight-thirty, breakfast at nine, followed by a walk exactly fifteen minutes later—try regularly doing each thing in order: first get up, then shower, then eat breakfast, then walk. When you know what's coming next, your brain is less likely to spiral into confusion. Then it can start to make sense of a chaotic world—and even a chaotic past.

Someone Who Gets You

Many years ago, a mentor of mine suggested that one mark of adulthood is not just learning how to get into relationships but how to gracefully exit them when they become unhealthy or beyond repair. Sometimes we, or the people around us, choose to blow things up or burn them down rather than letting them fade away, possibly as a way to feel some sense of control over the end. Sometimes we try to keep friendships going out of momentum or memory after they're no longer serving us well. Take stock of your friendships. It's okay to let some fade away, and it doesn't mean there is something wrong with you or your friends. Other times you may wonder whether some people might not want you to grow or change; they might consciously or unconsciously be holding you back, invested in the status quo of how and who you are in their own minds.

As you change and grow, new people, perspectives, and choices will enter your life. After you interact with someone in person, on the phone, or online, take time to reflect on who really brings you up, not down. This can be painful. The more we grow, the more we out-grow, and when that happens, we need to let go of old habits, old ideas, and even old friends to make room for the new, healthier people and ideas to come into our lives. A client's friend recently told her, "You haven't met everyone who will love you yet," a line that really stuck with her *and* me.

Because you do need people, ask, Who really gets you? Who can tolerate *all* of you? A partner, a friend, a therapist? My friend Mike used to say, "If you want to get better, you need just one person who you can be absolutely honest with." It was heart advice—and hard advice. I believe it still, and after Mike took his own life, I always wonder what secrets he held onto.

So who really gets you? You only need to start with one person, and remember that you may be that one person for someone else. And not everyone needs to be everything. It's okay—healthy even—to have that work friend who knows some part of you, that parent-ing friend who knows your struggle, that sadness friend, that friend you text during your favorite, guilty-pleasure TV show—so long as you move toward integration.

There's that saying that you are the average of the five people you spend the most time with. Trauma can keep our social life small to stay safe at first. When you are ready to expand, bring in more diversity and new perspectives; bring in people from different professions. By and large, I personally find a lot of therapists insufferable, and I try to broaden my social world to include artists and writers, anthropologists and economists who I think have as much or more to teach me about human nature and healing than many of my colleagues.

Also remember that online, you may be the average of the five people who post the most on your social media. If they, too, are struggling, you may watch them fall into negativity, miracle cures, conspiracy theories, and more as their best brains shut down. Moreover, social media algorithms feed you more conflict, clickbait, and negativity, and there is nothing wrong with hiding, blocking, and snoozing those people online. Trust me, it can make a huge difference. Even the people who show off how great their lives are might drive you bananas. Hide them, too, if they make you feel worse. And why not deliberately follow some inspiring people and accounts in your social media to override that negativity bias we all have?

Building stronger relationships can help you connect around the positive, the growth, and the solutions—not just the problems. As humans, it's easiest to connect around the negative. Social media companies know that's true, and the same applies offline. Most employees connect at work by complaining about their bosses; parents bitch on the playground about new school policies. This is what we humans do. To beat that negativity bias in your interactions, try to lead off and even sign off conversations with other topics. Ask: What books are you reading lately? What new recipes or restaurants have you enjoyed? What are you planning for vacation or staycation this year? These simple actions can quietly set boundaries around negativity and help start and end conversations on a positive note.

For Compassionate Conversations, THINK Before You Speak!

Trauma can make assertive and clear communication a challenge. When our brains are muddled by stress, it becomes harder to communicate clearly and effectively. Most of us have had the experience of saying something we regret, wishing the floor would swallow us whole, and momentarily hoping our yoga practice will let us literally insert our foot into our mouth. Other times, we struggle to find the right words to frame what we are saying, and we end up angry at ourselves for not speaking up. But beyond blunders and bloopers, we've all struggled to effectively communicate and be heard by others. So when and how can mindfulness and compassion really help?

Although mindfulness won't make us perfect communicators, it can settle the nervous system enough that we can ask with clarity, confidence, and compassion what our needs are. Mindful and compassionate speaking isn't just for the sake of being kind—it's simply more effective. A lot of mindfulness wisdom recommends reflecting on what we are about to say so that we can say it and be true, kind, gentle, and timely. Here, I've adapted the popular acronym THINK with some mindful variations.

THINK Before You Speak

Is it True? Is it Helpful? Am I the one to say it?
What are the Intentions and Impact?
Is it Necessary Now? Is it Kind?

T: *Is it true?* First we want to speak the truth. In this way, we avoid harming others, and we are also less likely to ensnare ourselves in a web of lies, mistruths, and the cognitive dissonance and guilt that come with them. Lying is uncomfortable; it actually activates the amygdala, which we know creates more stress.

At a more nuanced level, we want to speak important truths because in addition to helping us, they might inspire others. Saying what's "true" is more than the opposite of lying: it's the power to speak our truth—individually and collectively—and to speak truth to power. Speaking truth can lead to the political change we've seen in truth-and-reconciliation processes around the world and to restorative-justice work being done in many communities. Truth has also led to social change in the #MeToo movement and others in which survivors have inspired millions to speak their truths and shake the foundations of how our culture perpetuates abuse.

H: *Is it helpful?* Before we speak, we can reflect on whether what we say will actually be of benefit to anyone, including ourselves. Gossiping or bragging might be true, but it's rarely helpful and is often harmful to us and others. The same is true of certain kinds of feedback we might give to those around us. Although the words we choose might very well be true, they might not exactly be helpful. Is it helpful to offer yet another complaint?

I: *Am I the one to say it?* Sometimes we feel an impulse to speak, but it may be none of our business. Then again, this can be hard to discern. There may be situations in which we wonder if we are the one to speak up and say something, so as to be an "upstander" rather than a "bystander." Mindful and compassionate reflection helps us discern—as hard as it may be—when it is our job to speak up. Still, the challenge can come in knowing if we are being baited or trolled into a fruitless keyboard battle or dinner-table debate, which is when these other guidelines may help.

What is my intention, and what is my impact? Although the impact of our words may be unpredictable, we would do well to reflect on them and closely examine our intentions with our speech.

N: *Is it necessary? Is now the time?* We might ask ourselves if what we want to say is actually necessary in this moment. Keep in mind that timing is everything. Sometimes the most mindful speech is no speech at all: restraint of keyboard and tongue or simply bearing compassionate witness. What's more, when we don't speak for a minute or two, we're more likely to notice body language and facial microexpressions that might be far more revealing than words.

Silence is all too rare in our busy world, yet holding our tongue can create an opportunity for intimate moments. Also, it is during our silences and pauses in conversation that we create the space for budding insights and ideas to emerge. Neuroscientists have discovered that there's more brain activity during the silences in therapy sessions than when there is speaking.

K: *Is it kind?* In the end, a comment is best received if it's presented in a way that's patient and kind. When someone feels attacked, their fight-or-flight response overrides their ability to take in new information. Remember that under threat—real or imagined, physical or emotional— our brains shut down the areas where we get perspective, see the big picture, understand where someone else might be coming from, and access our critical interpersonal and communication skills. Using harsh words or tone may change how someone is acting in the moment, but it rarely creates effective, long-term change without collateral damage.

Another aspect of kindness to consider is whether our conversation is ultimately positive or negative. I've noticed in myself and others that it's often easier to default to negativity than positivity, as we discussed earlier. Here's a challenge: try paying attention to whether your regular interactions are more positive or more negative. The answer might surprise you. The old adage, "If you don't have anything nice to say, don't say anything at all," might also be worth examining. See what intimacy you find in silence. Research suggests that an incredible amount of brain activity happens during the silences in a conversation— perhaps even more than when we are speaking.

Also, speaking compassionately to ourselves is just as important as speaking confidently and compassionately in the real world. Can you work with your own inner voice around the THINK acronym as well?

The Compassion Contagion

As a mindfulness teacher, I'm often asked, What is the point of spending all of our time sitting in silence on a meditation cushion? To me, the point is not to get good at sitting still but to cultivate a deeper wisdom of when and how to move and act. The point is not to get good at being silent; we practice silence to get better at speaking up and speaking out when it's time to do that. I believe the mindfulness and meditation movements in the West have fallen short in building community and connection, although I do feel that we are starting to see more positive change in that direction.

Trauma can silence us, freeze our bodies, and isolate us, making practices like meditation seem even more questionable on their face. It can feel inherently disempowering—at least at first—to consider silence and stillness as a response to our distress. Overwhelming feelings of helplessness and vulnerability are the very symptoms we are hoping to treat. In the face of all this, how do we begin to feel the world is safe, and how do we begin to feel more empowered in it? If helplessness is a prominent symptom, what can we do about it? We can, as Mr. Rogers's mother famously suggested, "Look for the helpers" in frightening times. Find the helpers—the first responders, the medical professionals, the therapists, the people who believe us and support us—and deliberately thank them because they make the world a little better. Also try thanking the "people in your neighborhood": sanitation workers, mail carriers, delivery drivers. Ask a grocery clerk how their day is going, mean it, and wait for the response.

Better yet, we can *be* the helpers, even in our own small way. You may not have the expertise or training to be a paramedic or a therapist, but the best way to not feel helpless is to help. What's more, volunteering might help you discover newfound passions, rediscover old ones, or even assist you in transitioning into a new career. Reams of research from positive psychology backs service as one of the best ways to boost your mood, overall happiness, and life satisfaction. Volunteering also helps you feel less isolated and alone. In fact, finding meaning in service and contributing to something larger than one's self is one of the best predictors of resilience in people who have been through adverse childhood experiences.

So consider what helping could mean for you. Donate money if you have it, or time if you have that. If you're good at arts and designing, make signs or posters for a campaign or movement that's important for you. Love cooking? Share recipes online, teach friends to cook, or bring food to people who could use it. If you can write, compose short blogs offering wisdom and advice. Create artwork and share it at your local coffee shop or just with friends. Or mail it to distant, lonely relatives or even folks in prison. If your health is good, help a neighbor with yard work or taking out the trash. Offer to pick up groceries for friends, family, and strangers. Give blood. Volunteer at the local library or youth center by reading out loud or teaching kids mindfulness or music. If you're athletic, teach dance or yoga or basketball skills. Offer language lessons, start a book club, offer a writing class (online or in person). Good with tech? Plenty of people need help in that department, and less tech-savvy friends and relatives may need help setting up connections to long-distance loved ones, support systems, or networks. If you work in advertising or marketing, consider ways to get positive messages and information out to people who need it. Handy around the house? Show a friend how to repair that leaky faucet or broken cabinet hinge.

Simply put: to start feeling less helpless, help. Consider how you can use your unique skills for the benefit of a neighbor or friend, and you'll find that those feelings of helplessness begin to fade as your own resilience grows.

Post-Traumatic Growth to Be a Good Ancestor

The incredible thing about helping is that it has an exponential effect, rippling outward toward others. In fact, when we do something kind and generous, it may well come back around, the science says. We are likely to be compassionate when we feel safe and secure, but acting compassionately helps us feel safe, secure, and happy. It's hard to know where it all begins.

We used to think about only nature and nurture—genes or environment—with regard to our health and mental health. The relatively new field of epigenetics, however, has shaken up more than a century of genetic science. Simply put, epigenetics explores the way our genes express themselves in relation to our experiences. Through the epigenetic lens, we're learning that how we respond to the large and small stresses of life may impact our children and grandchildren at the genetic level. Our ancestors' experiences may have reshaped their DNA, which expressed itself in new ways that were passed down to us. Take a look at your family tree: many of our ancestors experienced war, slavery, genocide, bigotry, and/or poverty. These historic traumas and stresses may have altered the DNA we're now walking around with today. The way we respond to stress—with optimism or pessimism, fear or generosity—is likely to be shaped by these same genetic influences.

A team of researchers took some happy, well-adjusted, genetically identical mice and stressed out half of them. The stressed mice, not surprisingly, acted differently than the mice that lived a low-stress life of eating cheese, napping in sawdust, and doing low-impact hamster wheel workouts every day. When the researchers tested the stressed mice, they found parts of their DNA had actually activated as a result of the stress. What's more, those genetic and behavioral changes were passed down even to those mice's grandchildren, who were born with the genetic changes. As Dr. James Potash, who led a study of epigenetics at Johns Hopkins University, put it, "If you think of the stress system as preparing you for fight or flight, you might imagine that these epigenetic changes might prepare you to fight harder or flee faster the next time you encounter something stressful."

So maybe you have lived through some traumas but you got help, went to therapy, or worked on your demons before your DNA began to change its expression. Maybe you laughed with friends, got a good night's rest, ate a healthy breakfast, and pulled onto the highway feeling well regulated. Cortisol isn't jamming your system, and oxytocin is flowing, so you can use your entire brain and access compassion as you drive. Now someone cuts you off, honking and speeding past. And maybe you think about the other driver: *She might be rushing her sick child to the hospital.* So you go ahead and wave that other driver into the lane with a smile.

Just after that, some amazing things happen, inside and out. Your brain's neuroplasticity forges a new pathway, hardwiring the new habit, making it more likely you'll be kind and generous tomorrow, too. There's a boost of serotonin, which regulates mood and anxiety. You also get a dose of oxytocin—that warm, fuzzy "love" hormone that stays elevated for a few hours—and dopamine, another feel-good reward neurotransmitter that helps build habits. In other words, generosity and compassion regulate mood and anxiety and make us feel safe enough for compassion. We also feel good when we do a good deed, because we're activating and building the parts of our brains associated with connection and trust. We are truly acting our way into a new way of feeling and thinking.

The social contagion effect, observed by Emory University's James Fowler and Yale's Nicholas Christakis, shows that acts of kindness and generosity spread from one person to the next. In numerous studies, they demonstrated that merely observing acts of generosity inspires a ripple effect of "downstream reciprocity" in others up to three degrees of separation from you. Researchers have also observed many of the same neurotransmitters in both givers and receivers of kindness, although there's a greater amount in the givers. In one study, researchers asked subjects to spend five dollars either on themselves or someone else. To the surprise of the researchers and the subjects, those who gave away the five dollars felt better than those who spent the money on themselves. Neuroscientist Richard J. Davidson has said, "The best way to activate positive-emotion circuits in the brain is through generosity."

When you do something as simple and seemingly small as waving another driver to go ahead of you, you're happier and more optimistic. The people around you are also happier, and they like and admire you more, wanting to be around you more. Instead of sending mean genes onward to future descendants, you pass along resilient, regulated ones. Plus, your behavior ripples outward by at least three degrees of separation and downward by at least three generations via gene expression. And when you let that driver merge in front of you, they're more likely to buy flowers for their wife, who might give an extra cookie to the kids, who, in turn, give the dog a hug on their way to bed. In addition, your own children affect the people they know in a positive way, and someday they will pass on their happier, more resilient genes to the next generation and the next. This is truly the start of becoming a good ancestor, literally and figuratively.

Get the Urge to Merge

My friend Shireen inspired the idea for this practice. She sounds like a made-up person, but she's not. She's actually an atheist Muslim in Twelve-Step recovery, who attended a Catholic boarding school in Pakistan and who practices Buddhist meditation. She doesn't believe in any one religion, but she practices compassion in a simple way each day by letting one person go ahead of her in traffic. Not everyone, but just one person a day. Where I live, this qualifies you for either sainthood or an incredible afterlife or rebirth, depending on what you believe in.

Next time you drive somewhere, give Get the Urge to Merge a try. Just let that driver in. You'll make someone else's day, affecting their family and friends and maybe even some strangers, too. You'll make yourself happy as you rewire yourself and your offspring for greater resilience, optimism, and the ability to see new opportunities as they arise. You'll go home happy and spread that compassion contagion to your roommates or family or cats and beyond—maybe even across the generations through your genetic expression. And in that way, you'll change the world and even move the course of human evolution toward greater kindness and greater compassion, just by waving in that person in traffic.

Building Trust and Safety

I've heard trust described as the opposite of trauma. Yet *trust* can be a hard word. Developing trust often means pushing against what trauma pushes us toward, what our trauma thinks is safety.

Do you experience low self-esteem? Perform estimable acts in the world, as a friend recommends. Harsh with yourself or to yourself? Practice self-compassion. Does your life feel chaotic? Try some stillness with a meditation. Even in pain, you can ask yourself, *And What Else* is present? (AWE) by taking a mindful, appreciative moment to connect with what *isn't* painful. Feel like isolating? Reach out. Breath dysreg-ulated? Slow it down and regulate it. Body crumpled up? Stretch it outward and upward.

The late Zen master Thich Nhat Hanh said, "Some-times your joy is the source of your smile, but sometimes your smile is the source of your joy." The research affirms this is true. We override negative emotions and unhelpful habits by writing over them with new ones. Like a computer trash can, nothing is ever deleted until it is written over. What are the new responses you are going to write through your actions, starting today? Can you write a new story of trust?

As we learn to trust our bodies and our minds, we can continue to build trust in the world and in others through compassion, self-compassion, and action. It is through others that we test our reality and judg-ment, with others that our bodies settle down, and in connection with others that we learn to take the healthy relational risks that bring us closer to trust—trust in ourselves, our bodies, and the world.

FINAL THOUGHTS

In many support groups I've heard people say, "We will love you until you can love yourself." In other spiritual rooms I've heard more simply, "We love you; keep going." And that's what we can do: we can love ourselves and keep going forward. We may not forget, but we can reset, restart, and rebuild a life stronger for what we've been through.

No amount of emotional or spiritual work makes life painless, but it can give us strength, presence, and equanimity through hard times. I wrote much of this book during the pandemic, often in a chair next to my mother's bed as she was dying. Writing to a friend after her death, I explained, "After all the work I've done these past twenty years—all the research and all the writing personally and professionally—it still Just. Fucking. Hurts."

I'm grateful simply that I'm not making that pain too much worse for myself or anyone else, now or in the long term, because everything that happens ripples outward. We know that chaos can ripple, but so too can calm and compassion. This is where we begin to turn ourselves, and the world around us, toward growth and progress, growing stronger through trauma individually and collectively.

As we regulate our bodies and brains—as we co-regulate calm and compassion with others—the impact ripples outward. Therapist and activist Resmaa Menakem says, "Trauma decontextualized in a person looks like personality. Trauma decontextualized in a family looks like family traits. Trauma in a people looks like culture." When I first read that quote, I thought of all the awful ways trauma shapes us through PTSD. Over time, I also started to see those ways that trauma shapes us with post-traumatic growth and by creating beautiful new rituals and practices in individuals, families, and cultures.

Generosity, self-compassion, mindfulness—all of these are contagious. Parents who practice these attributes, even if their partners or their kids roll their eyes, make the whole family happier. There's better communication and fewer accidents in the home, and worrisome behavior decreases. Social skills and mood seem to improve, lifting up siblings, too. When one partner in a couple practices generosity, self-compassion, and mindfulness, both appear to be happier with the relationship, with less reactivity and conflict. Studies show that when one person meditated alternating weeks, their roommates, romantic partners, friends, and family members were happier during those weeks. So you really can raise the mood of the people around you by simply exploring these practices for yourself and by extending good vibes to your friends, family, and loved ones during hard times.

A couple of years ago I went back to visit and speak at a treatment center where I'd gotten a lot of help as a young man. Once I stopped crying in gratitude, I shared a bit about my own journey and about what had happened to the other guys from my time. Many I had lost touch with, and still others never made it, but the ones who did had something in common: they'd found meaning and purpose. For some that was religion and spirituality, but for others it was other things. The guy who was always cracking jokes ended up with a career in comedy. The friend who had been abused by a teacher at boarding school went on to become a renowned nature photographer. Another survivor of ruthless childhood bullying discovered that through teaching he could be there for children in a way that adults hadn't been there for him.

It's my wish for you that, as you finish this book, a few of these practices and ideas will resonate and you will find yourself on the path of post-traumatic growth simultaneously with post-traumatic stress. I hope that the seeds you are planting here lead to growth in your mind, body, and spirit. I hope you feel a greater sense of appreciation for life itself through practices like gratitude and mindfulness, along with appreciation of yourself and others through self-compassion and self-care. Remember, you don't have to run a marathon, climb a mountain, or start a movement. In fact, if you simply choose to keep moving forward, I hope you can see that your simple acts of resilience are acts of resistance toward those who would perpetuate more trauma in this world. My hope is that more people—the right people—enter your life to help you on this journey (or for part of it), and that by shifting toward a more mindful and compassionate approach to your life and the world, you will make room for greater meaning to arise.

CITATIONS BY CHAPTER

Chapter 1: Wired for Resilience

Dana, Deb. *Anchored: How to Befriend Your Nervous System Using Polyvagal Theory*. Boulder, CO: Sounds True, 2021.

Olff, Miranda. "Sex and Gender Differences in Post-Traumatic Stress Disorder: An Update." *European Journal of Psychotraumatology* 8, no. sup4 (July 27, 2017): 1351204. doi.org/10.1080/20008198.2017.1351204.

Porges, Stephen W. *The Polyvagal Theory: Neurophysiological Foundations of Emotions, Attachment, Communication, and Self-Regulation*. New York: W. W. Norton & Company, 2011.

Schwartz, Richard C. *No Bad Parts: Healing Trauma and Restoring Wholeness with the Internal Family Systems Model*. Boulder, CO: Sounds True, 2021.

Siegel, Daniel J. *The Developing Mind: How Relationships and the Brain Interact to Shape Who We Are*. 2nd ed. New York and London: Guilford Press, 2015.

Tedeschi, Richard G., and Bret A. Moore. *The Posttraumatic Growth Workbook: Coming Through Trauma Wiser, Stronger, and More Resilient*. Oakland, CA: New Harbinger Publications, 2016.

Chapter 2: Your Resilient Body

Bohns, Vanessa K., and Scott S. Wiltermuth. "It hurts when I do this (or you do that): Posture and pain tolerance." *Journal of Experimental Social Psychology* 48, no. 1 (2012): 341–45. doi.org/10.1016/j.jesp.2011.05.022.

Bos, Maarten W., and Amy J. C. Cuddy. "iPosture: The Size of Electronic Consumer Devices Affects Our Behavior." Harvard Business School working paper, May 20, 2013. dash.harvard.edu/bitstream/handle /1/10646419/13-097 .pdf?sequence=1&isAllowed=y. The authors also note: "In a separate study with one hundred participants, we showed that the smaller the device, the more contractive our posture: hands are closer together, shoulders are more slumped, and we're generally less expansive."

Cuddy, Amy. *Presence: Bringing Your Boldest Self to Your Biggest Challenges*. New York: Back Bay Books, 2018.

Harvard Medical School. "Regular Exercise Releases Brain Chemicals Key for Memory, Concentration, and Mental Sharpness." *Harvard Men's Health Watch*, May 1, 2013. https:// www.health.harvard.edu/press_releases/regular-exercise-releases -brain-chemicals-key-for-memory-concentration-and-mental -sharpness.

Keltner, Dacher. *Born to Be Good: The Science of a Meaningful Life*. New York: W. W. Norton & Company, 2009. Recommended information on touch research.

Mandolesi, Laura, Arianna Polverino, Simone Montuori, Francesca Foti, Giampaolo Ferraioli, Pierpaolo Sorrentino, and Giuseppe Sorrentino. "Effects of Physical Exercise on Cognitive Functioning and Wellbeing: Biological and Psychological Benefits." *Frontiers in Psychology* 9, no. 509 (April 27, 2018). doi.org/10.3389/fpsyg.2018.00509.

Neff, Kristin. "The Criticizer, the Criticized, and the Compassionate Observer" (an exercise). In *Self-Compassion: The Proven Power of Being Kind to Yourself*. (New York: William Morrow, 2011). See also the Supportive Touch Exercise on Dr. Neff's website: self-compassion.org/exercise-4-supportive-touch/.

Nestor, James. *Breath: The New Science of a Lost Art*. New York: Riverhead Books, 2020.

Nguyen, Anh-Huong, and Thich Nhat Hanh. *Walking Meditation: Easy Steps to Mindfulness.* Boulder, CO: Sounds True, 2019.

Nhat Hanh, Thich. *How to Eat.* Berkeley, CA: Parallax Press, 2014.

Parnell, Laurel. *Tapping In: A Step-by-Step Guide to Activating Your Healing Resources Through Bilateral Stimulation.* Boulder, CO: Sounds True, 2008.

Ratey, John J., and Richard Manning. *Go Wild: Eat Fat, Run Free, Be Social, and Follow Evolution's Other Rules for Total Health and Well-Being.* New York: Little, Brown and Company, 2015.

Sapolsky, Robert M. "Testicular Function, Social Rank, and Personality among Wild Baboons." *Psychoneuroendocrinology* 16, no. 4 (1991): 281–93. doi.org/10.1016/0306-4530(91)90015-l.

Seppälä, Emma M., Jack Nitschke, Dana L. Tudorascu, Andrea Hayes, Michael R. Goldstein, Dong T. H. Nguyen, David Perlman, Richard J. Davidson. "Breathing-Based Meditation Decreases Posttraumatic Stress Disorder Symptoms in U.S. Military Veterans: A Randomized Controlled Longitudinal Study." *Journal of Traumatic Stress* 27, no. 4 (August 26, 2014): 397–405. doi.org/10.1002/jts.21936.

Sharma, Ashish, Vishal Madaan, and Frederick D. Petty. "Exercise for Mental Health." *Primary Care Companion to the Journal of Clinical Psychiatry.* 8, no. 2 (2006): 106. omegamentalhealth.com/news/item/20-exercise-for-mental-health.html.

Wilson, Vietta E., and Erik Peper. "The Effects of Upright and Slumped Postures on the Recall of Positive and Negative Thoughts." *Applied Psychophysiology and Biofeedback* 29, no. 3 (September 2004): 189–95. doi.org/10.1023/b:apbi.0000039057.32963.34.

Chapter 3: Your Resilient Mind

Dana, Deb. *The Polyvagal Theory in Therapy: Engaging the Rhythm of Regulation.* New York: W. W. Norton & Company, 2018.

Hanson, Rick. "Take In the Good." Personal blog. Accessed [insert access date here]: rickhanson.net/take-in-the-good/.

Hayes, Steven C., and Spencer Smith. *Get Out of Your Mind and Into Your Life: The New Acceptance and Commitment Therapy.* Oakland, California: New Harbinger Publications, 2005.

Killingsworth, Matthew A., and Daniel T. Gilbert. "A Wandering Mind Is an Unhappy Mind." *Science* 330, no. 6006 (November 12, 2010): 932. doi.org/10.1126/science.1192439.

University of Pennsylvania Positive Strengths Inventory link: https://www.authentichappiness.sas.upenn.edu/

Chapter Four: Resilient Heart

Dana, Deb. *Befriending Your Nervous System: Looking Through the Lens of Polyvagal Theory.* Read by the author. Boulder, CO: Sounds True, 2020. Audible audio ed., 8 hr, 24 min.

Devine, Megan. *It's OK That You're Not OK: Meeting Grief and Loss in a Culture That Doesn't Understand.* Boulder, CO: Sounds True, 2018.

Dunbar, R. I. M. "Neocortex Size as a Constraint on Group Size in Primates." *Journal of Human Evolution* 22, no. 6 (June 1992): 469–93. doi.org/10.1016/0047-2484(92)90081-j.

Fowler, James H., and Nicholas A. Christakis. "Cooperative Behavior Cascades in Human Social Networks." *Proceedings of the National Academy of Sciences* 107, no. 12 (March 8, 2010): 5334–38. doi.org/10.1073/pnas.0913149107.

Germer, Christopher, and Kristin Neff. "The Mindful Self-Compassion Training Program." In T. Singer and M. Bolz. *Compassion: Bridging Theory and Practice*, 365–96. Munich, Germany: Max-Planck Institute, 2013.

hooks, bell. *Talking Back: Thinking Feminist, Thinking Black.* New York: Routledge, 2015.

National Institute on Aging. "Social Isolation, Loneliness in Older People Pose Health Risks." National Institute on Aging, April 23, 2019. nia.nih.gov/news/social-isolation-loneliness-older -people-pose-health-risks#:~:text=Research%20has%20linked %20social%20isolation.

Wein, Harrison. "Stress Hormone Causes Epigenetic Changes." National Institutes of Health/*NIH Research Matters*, September 27, 2010. https://www.nih.gov/news-events/nih -research-matters/stress-hormone-causes-epigenetic-changes.

Wood, Joanne V., W. Q. Elaine Perunovic, and John W. Lee. "Positive Self-Statements: Power for Some, Peril for Others." *Psychological Science* 20, no. 7 (July 2009): 860–66. doi.org/10 .1111/j.1467-9280.2009.02370.x.

Final Thoughts

Menakem, Resmaa. *My Grandmother's Hands: Racialized Trauma and the Pathway to Mending Our Hearts and Bodies.* London: Penguin Books, 2021.

Menakem, Resmaa. *My Grandmother's Hands: Racialized Trauma and the Pathway to Mending Our Hearts and Bodies.* (Las Vegas, NV: Central Recovery Press, 2017).

ACKNOWLEDGMENTS

E ach book I finish, it feels like all I've done is share and sometimes build on the wisdom of others, just in a neatly assembled package. This book is, again, simply the integration of a much greater wisdom and science that has come before me, which I've measured and baked into this book in your hands. So many remarkable individuals and conversations shaped this book, in addition to the contributions of strangers I've never met.

I first want to thank my mentor, colleague, and friend Chris Germer, who has pioneered so much amazing work in self-compassion, and his frequent collaborator Kristen Neff.

Many friends and colleagues generously shared their time, research, and wisdom with me. Deb Dana spent an hour, at least, on Zoom with me explaining polyvagal theory, while David Treleaven and Linda Graham spent Zoom calls with me discussing trauma and resilience. Long pandemic phone calls with Dr. Sará King, Caverly Morgan, and Leslie Booker sparked new inspirations and perspectives, all of whom became new friends and colleagues somehow during the pandemic and with hardly an in-person interaction.

Likewise thanks to Leanna Rae, whose wonderful conversations sparked so many ideas, along with my frequent collaborator Mitch Abblett, and my friend Ashley Vigil-Otero. I am also so grateful for the vulnerability of conversations with my new friend Anne Marie Miller, current friends Amelia and David, and my old friend Paul, who offered to share their experiences and wisdom as well.

Ron Siegel, Ethan Nichtern, Ed Yeats, and Joe Shay also always offer sage wisdom and advice, alongside humorous perspectives on the craziness of writing and publishing and speaking and therapizing.

Many other teachers play a role in this book, and are in the text: Rick Hanson, Emma Seppälä, Amy Cuddy, Brian Callahan, Jessica Morey, Dan Siegel, and so many others.

Thank you of course, too, to my friends and family who have contributed so much; thank you mom and dad, Olivia, Leo, and Mae for your patience and your curiosity.

And of course I can't thank Sounds True and Tami Simon enough for believing in what I cannot believe is my seventh book with them, and for the wonderful editorial support of Jennifer Yvette Brown.

Most of all, thank you to my friends, students, colleagues, and most of all my students and my clients who trusted me to share their stories with me, and trusted my sharing these practices with them.

ABOUT THE AUTHOR

Dr. Christopher Willard, (Psy. D.) is a clinical psychologist, author and consultant. He has led workshops live in more than two dozen countries, and has presented at two TEDx events. He is the author of twenty books, including *Alphabreaths* (2019), *Growing Up Mindful* (2016) and many more. His thoughts on mental health have been featured in The New York Times, The Washington Post, mindful.org, cnn.com, and elsewhere. He lives in Cambridge, Massachusetts with his family and teaches at Harvard Medical School.

ABOUT SOUNDS TRUE

Sounds True is a multimedia publisher whose mission is to inspire and support personal transformation and spiritual awakening. Founded in 1985 and located in Boulder, Colorado, we work with many of the leading spiritual teachers, thinkers, healers, and visionary artists of our time. We strive with every title to preserve the essential "living wisdom" of the author or artist. It is our goal to create products that not only provide information to a reader or listener but also embody the quality of a wisdom transmission.

For those seeking genuine transformation, Sounds True is your trusted partner. At SoundsTrue.com you will find a wealth of free resources to support your journey, including exclusive weekly audio interviews, free downloads, interactive learning tools, and other special savings on all our titles.

To learn more, please visit SoundsTrue.com/freegifts or call us toll-free at 800.333.9185.

sounds true
WAKING UP THE WORLD